HOW TO BE HAPPY

IT'S YOUR DIVINE DESTINY

JOHN MARINELLI

How to be Happy
Ocala, Florida 1/4/2023 by John Marinelli.
All rights reserved.
First Edition 2023

Print ISBN # 978-1-0880-8186-0
eBook ISBN # 978-1-08/80-8187-7

"How to be happy" is protected by the United States copyright laws. Any reproduction or use whatsoever is prohibited unless authorized by the author in writing.

More books and Christian Ministry at: www.marinellichristianbooks.com

PREFACE

"How to be Happy" is a journey to find true happiness which is our Divine destiny. It is also a Biblical teaching that reveals the truths of God's Word and how we can apply them to our lives. We will read from the Psalms about the Joy of the Lord as well as hear what the Old Testament prophets and New Testament apostles had to say about being happy.

We will explore the concept of joy and lasting peace in a world full of turmoil. The King James version of the Bible will be used in most cases to quote scripture passages.

The knowledge and practical applications presented represent the author's walk with God and relationship with the Holy Spirit over the last 60 years. It is his hope that his readers will grow spiritually as they follow after lasting peace and true happiness.

TABLE OF CONTENTS

Preface	iii
Introduction	1
Chapter One: Happiness By Design	3
Chapter Two: Happiness By Choice	17
Chapter Three: Happiness By Relationship	24
Chapter Four: Happiness Through God's Holy Spirit	37
Chapter Five: Happiness And Persecution	54
Chapter Six: Happiness Through Resting	64
Chapter Seven: There Is a Reason for Everything	76
Chapter Eight: Staying Happy 24/7	87
Chapter Nine: Hindrances To Being Happy	97
Conclusion	100
About The Author: John Marinelli	102
Gallery of Encouraging Poems	103

INTRODUCTION

Everyone wants to be happy. Don't you agree? I cannot imagine an individual ever saying that they enjoy sadness or misery. Isn't living one big quest for the good life?

Most of us strive for something, we don't know what, but think it is something that will satisfy or fill the void in our souls.

I graduated high school about 60 years ago. Back then, we all spoke of being somebody one day. Some said they wanted to be wealthy. Some said they wanted to settle down and have a family. Some said they wanted a position of power so they could change the world. In every case, we all spoke of being happy and fulfilled. Nobody said they wanted to be a drunk, a prostitute, a drug addict, a burglar, a child molester or any bad type of person.

Back in 1963, after graduation, we all started our individual searches for that one thing that would make us happy. We never thought that there was more than one thing. It was always that one thing that would cash in to be our savior.

It's been a long journey for me. I tried the power route and the quest for riches and even a family. But it seemed that everything I sought after faded away, broke apart or was just out of my reach. That is, until I met my current wife. It's been over 40-years now and we are still madly in love. February 2023 will be 41 years.

I quickly realized that the world system of living does not hold the answer to life's most sought-after treasure, happiness. What we seek after just doesn't provide a lasting happiness when or if we attain it. However, the Bible does offer really good answers.

The Bible says, *"Love not the world, neither the things that are in the world. If any man loves the world, the love of the Father is not in him. For all that is in the world, the lust of the flesh, and the lust of the eyes, and the pride of life, is not of the Father, but is of the world. And the world passes away, and the lust thereof: but he that does the will of God abides forever."* I John 2:15-17

I heard a preacher once that taught on this passage in I John. He spoke of this, *"Love not the world"* statement as if the world, with all its things, was no more than an old house that the city had condemned. It was set to be demolished. It was still standing but not for long.

The preacher said, "What would happen if you decided to take up residence in that old building and maybe even start to fix it up so it would be more livable? The condemning decree has already been declared. An entirely new structure will replace the old house on the foundation where it once stood.

Wouldn't all the work and money you spent be in vain? So would all those precious hours you used up on something that would never last. That's what the apostle John meant when he told the 1st century Christians that this world was like the old house. It was going to pass away. It wasn't worth their time and effort.

John pointed his flock to something that they could do that would last far beyond their lifetime. You know what that one thing was? Yep! *It was doing the will of God.*

CHAPTER ONE:
HAPPINESS BY DESIGN

Did you know that your happiness was planned before the world was? It is part of God's destiny for mankind. He wants us to be happy. Thus, comes the revelation of himself and his will so we have a guide to follow. Therefore, it only makes sense that by doing the will of God we will find happiness. You may ask:

1. How, exactly does that happen?
2. How do we know we are doing the will of God?
3. Is there an instruction manual or cheat sheet that we can look at and know for sure?

Yes, there is. It's called the Holy Bible. We can find the answers to most of our questions in the Scriptures. That's where I found Jesus, or should I say, "He found me." Hear what he said, *"The thief comes only to steal and kill and destroy.* **I have come that they may have life,** *and* **have it** *in all its fullness"*. John 10:10

I began to read and suddenly, without any prompting or manipulation, came words of wisdom that I could use in decision making. There were also promises made to the children of Israel that I could apply to my life situations. I even discovered instructions that the New Testament apostles gave to the early church. All of this led me to a place of assurance that I was indeed doing the will of God. Here's a few examples:

A prudent (or wise) man foresees evil and hides himself; The simple pass on and are punished. Proverbs 27:12 NKJ I saw this scripture as a wakeup call: that I should be aware of evil and not put myself in its path…to stay away from that which I know to be wrong.

Happy is he that condemns not himself in that thing which he allows. Romans 14:22b Living with yourself, when no one is around, can be difficult if you are constantly going against your own conscience. There is no peace, only confusion, guilt and a sense of not being worthy of God's love.

On the other hand, doing the will of God, as you know it, brings peace and even joy to your life experiences. It lifts up the soul and sets it on higher ground where you can fellowship with the Lord through his Holy Spirit.

It makes me feel better and keeps me positive, even when I go through tough times…because I know that I am right with my Creator. He is the only one that I have to please and that is more valuable to me than silver or gold or the praise of those around me.

I know that some will want further explanation to better understand this mindset so, I will elaborate in hopes of making myself absolutely clear.

Most of us live our lives based upon assumptions that may or may not be true. Some folks don't even question the thought process that society says is the basis for living. They say that there is no "Real Truth" anymore. It seems to be your truth or my truth but never *Absolute Truth*. I guess that is why so many folks are confused and have difficulty trying to figure out their existence. The truth seems to elude them.

I believe that **"Absolute Truth"** comes from God and is revealed in the Bible. In order to be really happy, we must know God's truth concerning our existence; we must ask ourselves three basic questions and look to the scriptures for the answers. Our conclusions will literally determine the way we live our lives here on earth and what our eternal destiny will be. They are also the basis for our everyday perspectives.

Life's Most Important Questions:
1. Where did I come from?
2. Why am I here?
3. What happens to me when I die?

We answer these questions based upon what truth we subscribe to. Our lives are built on what we believe. Our actions are determined by how we think.

There is a Bible verse that illustrates my point. Hear what Jesus said.

"Everyone then who hears these words of mine and does them will be like a wise man who built his house on the rock. And the rain fell, and the floods came, and the winds blew and beat on that house, but it did not fall, because it had been founded on the rock. And everyone who hears these words of mine and does not do them will be like a foolish man who built his house on the sand. And the rain fell, and the floods came, and the winds blew and beat against that house, and it fell, and great was the fall of it. Therefore, whosoever hears these sayings of mine, and doeth them, I will liken him unto a wise man, which built his house upon a rock" Mathew 7: 24 (Story thru v-27)

There are always two paths to walk, two roads to follow, and two choices in life for every decision. The choice we make could very well be the destruction of our home, family and lifestyle. To be like the wise man, we must decide to follow Jesus and build our existence and future on him.

Knowing what God says is true and applying it will always keep us in times of trouble. So it is in this life. We must know the answers to life's most important questions and apply them in order to be happy and fulfilled as a person. To do otherwise is a self-deception that will steal our destiny and condemn us to a life of Hell.

The 1st question is, "Where Did We Come From?"

Over the past 60 years, we have been deceived into thinking that we came into existence as a result of evolution. (God's **"Absolute Truth"** was replaced by man's ungodly theory.)

Evolution says there is no God and all that exist is a result of random selection. Some *"Think-tanks"* will acknowledge the existence of a god but will not ascribe any personality to it or active interaction with creation. It is true that various chemicals exist, however, that doesn't mean they can evolve, on their own, into any kind of life. That's like saying if I put the parts of a car in a garage and let them simmer for a million or billion years, they will evolve, on their own, into a fully operational vehicle.

Life is more than a mixture of chemicals. Random Selection cannot produce anything more than gobbledygook.

Man Is & Always Will Be A Special Creation

A friend of mine told me a true story of a man that found a large egg in his field. He took it into his chicken coup and put it under a chicken who sat on it until it hatched. The result was an eagle. It grew and pecked in the barnyard like a chicken. It never flew like an eagle the way it was supposed.

This story is a good example of human beings that were created to be like an eagle being empowered by God to soar into the heavens and glide over the earth. They are eagles that do not know they are eagles. They live and act like chickens because the chickens taught them to be a chicken. Society does that to us. It dictated who we are and why we are here. It tells us that we are not an eagle but just a silly old chicken.

The Bible tells us that God created man. **That's where we came from.** Life does not make any sense unless we are *God's Special Creation*. He chose to form man out of the dust of the earth and he breathed into him the breath of life, **which was his own life force,** his Holy Spirit. God's life caused man to become alive, *a living soul*. Here's the supporting text.

*"And the LORD God formed man of the dust of the ground, **and breathed into his nostrils** the breath of life; **and man became a living soul.**"* **Genesis 2:7**

The very definition of life, from a Biblical perspective, is being joined spiritually with our creator. We must have his life in us to be a living soul. Those who do not have his *"breath of life"* in them are no more than the walking dead.

A Living Soul

The human soul is a combination of *Mind, Will and Emotion*. This is where we reason, make decisions and feel. The wonder of it all is seen in the fact that man can operate within his soul separate from God. He can exist and control his own destiny.

The problem with that is…God never wanted man to exist separate from him. His plan was that they walk together in this life. He indwelled man and empowered him to live on a Godly plane of existence where he could be blessed and loved.

True life and happiness is when man is indwelled with God's Spirit. This connects God with man and man with God. Man does not really live without God. He may exist but not as a living soul.

Being A Special Creation

If we are honest with each other, we can admit that there are many times that we do not feel special and wonder why it is that God created us. What's so special that we should marvel at our existence?

The difference between man and the rest of creation is that man was made in the image and likeness of God.

If we study the account of man's creation and his sin against his creator, we immediately realize that Adam lost the image and likeness of God when he sinned. Instead, he took on the very nature of evil. Let me show you from the scriptures.

"Therefore, just as sin came into the world through one man, and death through sin, and so death spread to all men because all sinned—**Romans 5:12** (This is a reference to Adam's Original Sin), **Therefore**, as one trespass led to condemnation for all men, so one act of righteousness leads to justification and life for all men. For as by the one man's disobedience, the many were made sinners, so by the one man's obedience, the many will be made righteous. **Romans 5:12, 18 & 19 kjv**

The above scriptures tell us that sin entered the world by and through the transgression of Adam, the first man. It also tells us that Adam's descendants took on the nature of sin. The breath of life from God was taken from Adam. He spiritually died or was cut off from God.

Adam's Transgression

When we transgress, we go beyond the limits imposed upon us by law, command or other statute. Speeding is going beyond the legal limit imposed by law. So it was with Adam. He went beyond the command of God. The Bible calls it disobedience.

Adam decided to ignore God's command and do his own thing. His rebellion led him into a realm void of God's love and grace. He became the lord over his own life and crowned himself as his own god. This attitude became the basis of the *"Sin Nature"* that passed on to his descendants and is what rules our world today. It is a, **"Do Your Own Thing,"** philosophy.

In **Genesis 2:17** God tells Adam regarding the tree of the knowledge of good and evil, *"in the day that you eat from it you shall surely die."* The saying that Adam would die was a Spiritual death that occurred at the moment he ate from the tree? Adam physically died 930 years later.

God never wanted Adam to know evil. His plan for mankind was only good. We were created by God so we could do his thing, not ours.

God's Thing

All the good, the blessings, the joys of life and our eternal destiny are wrapped up in *"God's Thing."* This proves out as seen in other Biblical accounts where Adam no longer walked continually in God's Spirit. He instead encountered another nature in

himself that was contrary to the will of God.

We can understand the sudden appearance of a new destructive nature in Adam by considering a pregnant girl that is a drug addict who has a baby while on drugs and discovers that her baby is also an addict. The addiction passed on to the child.

So it is with the sin nature. It was passed on from Adam to his descendants down through the ages. Thus, all are infected. All have sinned. God's special creation was cut off from its creator and God's desire to fellowship on his level with man was lost. God lost the image of himself in the earth and man lost his Spiritual bond with God.

But the story doesn't end here. There is more. It's called, "The Gospel" or "Good News"

So we, as the descendants of Adam, are a fallen race that is in need of redemption. However, God did not cast us off. He restored his image and likeness in man through the cross of Jesus Christ.

Jesus paid the penalty for our sins and lived the life we should have lived before God. That's why he is our savior. That's why he is the only way to God. No other man could qualify because they are all of a fallen nature and in need of a savior.

Some folks reject the sacrificial death of Christ for the sins of mankind saying that he was also a descendant of Adam and therefore equally guilty of sin. However, they forget that **Jesus was born of a virgin.** He escaped the sin nature that passed on to humanity through Adam. His unique birth qualified him to become the spotless Lamb of God that God required as the ultimate sacrifice.

We are forgiven because Jesus died in our stead and we are accepted because Jesus never sinned. His righteousness is imputed into us and his blood cleanses us from all unrighteousness. It's as though we had never sinned. Listen to what Jesus said as recorded by the apostle John.

"For God so loved the world, that he gave his only begotten Son, that whosoever believeth in him should not perish, but have everlasting life" John 3:16

The Apostle John tells us, *"If we confess our sins, he is faithful and just to forgive us our sins, and to cleanse us from all unrighteousness."* **I John 1:9**

Once the blood of Jesus cleanses us from all sin, (unrighteousness), and we are saved by his life, we can rest assured that indeed, we are a Special Creation of God.

Here's what the Apostle Paul said.

"That if thou shalt confess with thy mouth the Lord Jesus, and shalt believe in thine heart that God hath raised him from the dead, thou shalt be saved. For with the heart man believeth unto righteousness; and with the mouth confession is made unto salvation." **(Romans 10:9-10)**

Knowing this gives us self-worth, no matter who accuses us or tells us different. We are his creation and his beloved. *"For we are his workmanship, created in Christ Jesus unto good works, which God hath before ordained that we should walk in them."* **Ephesians 2:10** We are the eagle, not the chicken and we can fly and even soar above all the evil and sorrow of this world.

Being happy is to know that God created us with himself in mind. He wanted and still does want a relationship with us. We are indeed his special.creation.

The 2nd question is Why Are We Here?

Some folks actually killed themselves because they could not figure out what life was all about. Suicide… says that there is "No Point to Life", "That we have no value as an individual", "That life has no meaning" Why Are We Here? Here are some Suicide statistics.

American Foundation for Suicide Prevention

Facts About Suicide in the US
- The annual age-adjusted suicide rate is **12.93 per 100,000** individuals.
- Men die by suicide **3.5x** more often than women.
- On average, there are **117** suicides per day.
- White males accounted for **7 of 10** suicides in 2014.
- Firearms account for **almost 50%** of all suicides.
- The rate of suicide is **highest in middle age**.
- Over **20 veterans kill** themselves every day.
- On average, 1 person commits suicide every 16- minutes.
- Untreated Depression is the number one cause of suicide.
- There are 2 times as many deaths due to suicide than AIDS.

For every suicide there are 25 attempted Suicides at a cost of $44 Billion annually.

Most adults are still searching for an identity, even into their senior years. They go through life holding on to titles as a way of explaining who they are. Without a title to define their existence they are lost and many loose interest in life.

The Used-To-Be Scenario

We live about 30 minutes north of The Villages, a huge retirement community. I know a lot of folks from that area. I hear some of them saying, "I used to be" or "I was" but rarely do I hear, "I AM". Some folks seem to have lost their identity and, in the process, themselves. More than 7,500 seniors took their own lives in 2014.

We were created in the image and likeness of God. **Genesis 1:27** records the event.

"And God created man in his own image, in the image of God created he him; male and female created he them." Here's what Jesus said about why he came to earth.

"The thief cometh not, but for to steal, and to kill, and to destroy: I am come that they might have life, and that they might have it more abundantly." **John 10:10**

We can live an abundant life. This is a life that is full of blessings, love and forgiveness. It is what Jesus wanted for us and made available to all who trust in him. He wanted us to be happy. He wants us to realize that we are eagles and can soar to heights unknown. It's time for us to stop pecking with the chickens and act like the eagles that God made us to be.

"Take therefore no thought for the morrow: for the morrow shall take thought for the things of itself. Sufficient unto the day is the evil thereof." Mathew 6:34

Remember that God is in control of the lives of those that are submitted to his love and care. His power is greater than anyone or anything.

Thinking about what we should wear, eat or do, in a worrisome way, is not good for us. It says that we do not trust God or believe that he is really able to meet our needs.

Taking no thought is to rest in the Master's provision and love. Verse 33 of Matthew chapter six tells us how to accomplish this task. *"But seek ye first the kingdom of God, and His righteousness, and all these things shall be added unto you"*

A Purpose Driven Life

God had a purpose for us in his creation. We were not just a random selection without a reason to exist. It was to bear his image and likeness in the earth. God is a Spirit, as the Bible tells us. It says that the image and likeness of God is not a physical resemblance but rather Spiritual. He wanted us to be the embodiment of his character, which is ... ***"Love, Peace, Joy, Longsuffering, Meekness, Gentleness, Self-Control, Goodness and Faith." Galatians 5:22-23***

Unfortunately, we see more anger, hate, murder, jealousy, and other evil deeds flowing from the hearts of our fellowman. When abortion is deemed as a health issue instead of murder, we know that the image of God has been lost.

Over 50 million babies have been killed in the womb since the Rowe vs. Wade decision. This is not what God intended. We were not created to kill our unborn in the name of good health.

We were created by God to show forth his glory and to have fellowship with him. He is the only true and living God. What we do in life as a profession should not exclude God. We are, after all, his image and likeness. We can reflect God's glory as workers, retirees, housewives, children or whatever we choose to do or be... as long as our light is shining bright with the Love of God. ***This is why we were placed upon this earth at this moment in time.*** This is the abundant life. This is how we become happy.

The 3rd question is Where Are We Going When We Die?

Do you remember the story when Jesus was telling his disciples that he was going away? (Referring to his death on the cross) Here's the account.

Simon Peter said unto him, Lord, where goes thou? Jesus answered him, where I go, thou canst not follow me now; but thou shalt follow me afterwards. Peter said unto him, Lord, why cannot I follow thee now? I will lay down my life for thy sake. **John 13:36-37**

Later he would tell Phillip, **John 14:6** *"I am the way, the truth, and the life: no man cometh unto the Father, but by me."*

All roads do not lead to Rome, nor do all religions lead us to eternal life. Paul said, *"Neither is there salvation in any other: for there is none other name under heaven given among men, whereby we must be saved."* **Acts 4:2**

Do not think that you can get into heaven through a church, a religious leader, a set of rules and regulations, or a doctrine that is contrary to what the apostles taught.

Hear what the Scriptures say about that. *"For if he that cometh preaches another Jesus, whom we have not preached, or if ye receive another spirit, which ye have not received, or another gospel, which ye have not accepted, ye might well bear with him."* **II Corinthians 11:4**

God is for us! He is not against us!

Note: To bear with him is to indulge or put up with or accept, which should not be done. The inference is that they should immediately be rejected as liars and false teachers. Those that follow such teachers will also suffer the judgment ascribed to them by God.

Our Future Home

"In my Father's house are many mansions: if it were not so, I would have told you. I go to prepare a place for you. And if I go and prepare a place for you, I will come again, and receive you unto myself; that where I am, there ye may be also." **John 14:2-3**

Jesus is the only way to God; the Father and he is even now engaged in the preparation of an eternal dwelling place for those who believe in him.

The Promise of God to the "Whosevers" In This World *"For God so loved the world, that he gave his only begotten Son, that whosoever believeth in him should not perish, but have everlasting life."* **John 3:16**

I decided long ago that I was one of those, **"Whosevers"** and I did what Jesus said in **John 3:16**, …

- I believed in Jesus as the only begotten Son of God.
- I believed that Jesus was indeed the only way to God the Father, who created me.
- I believed that Jesus came to earth to die for my sins so I could have victory over death, hell and the grave.
- I believed that Jesus rose from the dead on the 3rd day as the scriptures declare.
- I believed that he prepared a place for me with him in heaven.

I am spending my senior years looking for my Savior to return and take me to my new home.

I am doing just fine, **but… what about you?** I want to invite you, **"All of You"** that read this book, to come into a saving knowledge of Jesus Christ. If you are not filled with the image and likeness of God, your creator, you need to be. He will wash away your sin and recreate you into a new creation that reflects his love and grace. You just need to repent and ask him to save you.

You can know the joy of being saved, of walking with God in this life and being assured of life after death when your time comes. **Hebrews 9:27** says, *"And as it is appointed unto men once to die, but after this the judgment"*

Please join me in being the **"Whosoever"** of **John 3:16** and discovering the joy of being saved. He will never let you down.

Where Are You Going When You Die?

There is only one true answer that brings happiness and an abundant life here on earth and in eternity. That answer is…*we will be with Jesus.* See it for yourself in the scriptures.

"For we know that if our earthly house of this tabernacle were dissolved, we have a building of God, an house not made with hands, eternal in the heavens. For in this we groan, earnestly desiring to be clothed upon with our house, which is from heaven: If so be that being clothed we shall not be found naked. For we that are in

this tabernacle do groan, being burdened: not for that we would be unclothed, but clothed upon, that mortality might be swallowed up of life.

Now he that hath wrought us for the selfsame thing is God, who also hath given unto us the earnest of the Spirit. 6 Therefore we are always confident, knowing that, whilst we are at home in the body, we are absent from the Lord: (For we walk by faith, not by sight:) 8 We are confident, I say, and willing rather to be absent from the body, and to be present with the Lord." **2-Corinthians 5:1-8**

Receive him today and his Holy Spirit will fill you with the image and likeness of God. You will be happy no matter what.

Believing in God is actually a mindset or perspective that has to be developed over time and through experiencing the trials of life. I know that my Lord is pleased with me. It's a great place to be. This is the ultimate happiness.

CHAPTER TWO:
HAPPINESS BY CHOICE

Being happy is your choice, no matter what is going on around you. God gave you a free will to make choices and happiness is one of those life choices you can make.

Let's look at free will and the sovereignty of God. He gave you a free will to be happy. He is not going to make you happy against your will. However, he will work with you to give you the desires of your heart. *"Delight Thyself Also in the Lord: and He Shall Give Thee the Desires of Thine Heart"* Psalm 37:4

Some folks feel that if God allows it, it is his fault. Is what's going on really his fault or yours? Who do we blame? Your happiness hangs in the balance.

Am I in control of my own destiny or is it all planned out and I am just a pawn in a much larger scheme? Sometimes I feel like I have no control over my life. Do you feel that way? This chapter will deal with "Free Will" verses the Sovereignty of God. This has been a source of controversy in the church for centuries. Is God in control, or am I the master of my own destiny?

The Sovereignty of God is the Biblical teaching that all things are under God's rule and control, and that nothing happens without his permission and direction. This view is supported by scripture.

Here's the text…God works, not just some things, but all things, according to the counsel of his own will (see Eph. 1:11). His purposes are all-inclusive and never thwarted (see Isa. 46:11); nothing takes him by surprise. The sovereignty of God is not merely that God has the power and right to govern all things, but that he does so, always, without exception. In other words, God is not merely sovereign in principle, but is also sovereign in practice.

"Although the sovereignty of God is universal and absolute, it is not the sovereignty of blind power. It is coupled with infinite wisdom, holiness, and love. This doctrine, when properly understood, is most comforting and reassuring. Who would not prefer to have his or her affairs in the hands of a God of infinite power, wisdom, holiness and love, rather than to have them left to fate, or chance, or irrevocable natural law, or to shortsighted and perverted self? Those who reject God's sovereignty should consider what alternatives they have left." Loraine Boettner.

God created all beings including the angels but some have fallen. Let us be sure that this does not make God the author of sin, for, as man, they fell from their created state. This includes all false gods. But God is over them, whether they be angels, demons, or the god of this world, the devil. The Psalmist said, "..*Thou are exalted far above all gods"*, Psalm 97:9, and again, ".. *Our Lord is above all gods,*" Psalm 135.5, and also *"O give thanks unto the God of gods."* Psalm 136.2.

Man may fight against God but cannot win over him. He often uses evil man to accomplish his will in the battle. Jesus is said to have been slain from the foundation of the world, and the cross is one of the most credible evidences of Gods Sovereignty. "Crucify him," "Crucify him", was their cry, but when they nailed him to the cross, they did not realize they were fulfilling God's will for his Son. Peter said, *"Him (Christ), being delivered by the determinate counsel and foreknowledge of God, ye have taken and by wicked hands have crucified and slain."* Acts 2:23.

But this God of all power was not defeated by this evil act, for the Lord Jesus was raised from the dead. By it the devil was defeated and all his ministers of (self)- righteousness. This is also a great example of Sovereignty and free will operating at the same time.

Judas, the one who betrayed Jesus, had betrayed himself, and met his just due. John wrote, *"Jesus knew from the beginning…who should betray him."* And he still said, *"no man can come unto me, except it were given unto him of my Father. Have not I chosen you twelve, and one of you is a devil (i.e., slanderer) … He spoke of Judas … for he it was that should betray him, being one of the twelve."* (John 6:64-71.) Our God cannot fail, lie, or sin. Neither is he frustrated at man's failure.

Judas exercised his own, "Free Will" in an act of betrayal but in doing so he played right into the hands of God that proclaimed even before the foundation of the world that Jesus, the Son of God, would be betrayed and slain. This act of betrayal took Jesus to the cross as the spotless Lamb of God in a divine sacrifice for the sins of the entire world. (Free Will & Sovereignty working hand-n-hand to accomplish the plan of God.)

God is the author of his sovereign grace and mercy. *"For he saith to Moses, I will have mercy on whom I will have mercy, and I will have compassion on whom I will have compassion. So, it is not of him that wills, nor of him that runs, but of God that shews mercy… And whom he will, he hardens."* (Rom. 9:15-16, 18.)

Many Christians have doubts about God's sovereignty, yet there is one aspect of the Christian life where they profess, maybe unknowingly, that God is sovereign. They may say, as many do, "God has done all he can do, now the rest is up to me."

How contradictory! They may stand on their feet and deny this blessed, comforting, enabling doctrine, but when they bend the knees in prayer, asking God to save, do they not realize they are calling on a sovereign God, who only he has the right and the ability to save?

The question is, If God has done all that he can do, why pray to him? But we pray knowing he is the only one who can do what man cannot otherwise do. This power belongs to God, and not man. (Excerpts from Sovereign Grace Baptist Proclaimer)

Now that you have a clearer understanding of the Sovereignty of God, let's talk more about the Free Will of man. It's important to see that man is not sovereign. He is rarely in control of the events that shape his life. However, God has still given man "Free Will" so he can choose his own lifestyle. In effect, we can be evil, nice, straight, gay or be and do anything we want. Our choices, however, comes with consequences. *"Be not deceived; God is not mocked: for whatsoever a man soweth, that shall he also reap."* (Gal. 6:7)

Pastor Steve Weaver writes, "A good definition of free will is the ability of the mind to make choices in accordance with its nature." Our nature is evil. Thus, we are bound by it in making choices. We choose the path that best suits our needs, even if it is in direct opposition to God's laws of righteousness.

This definition of "free will" also applies to God's free will. He too is bound by his nature. Therefore, he cannot sin! Why? Because it is not his nature! But God does have a free will and, unlike human beings, he has an accompanying good and holy nature.

Jonathan Edwards, a 17th century Christian preacher and theologian said that the will is the mind choosing: though there is a distinction between mind and will, the two are inseparable in action. We do not make a choice without our mind approving that choice. We choose according to our strongest inclination at any given moment.

The Bible teaches that I'm not free to choose God because it is contrary to my nature. That's why we need new natures that are given to us by the Holy Spirit at regeneration. *Unless a man is "Born Again" he cannot enter or even see the kingdom of God"* (John 3).

Though man is commanded to seek the Lord while he may be found, and to come to Christ, we watch in vain for man to do so. Romans 3:11

literally reads, "There is no God seeker." John 6:44 says, *"No one can come to me, (Jesus), unless the Father who sent me draws him and I will raise him up on the last day."* Literally, the verse says, *"no one is able."*

Gerhard Kittel's Theological Dictionary of the New Testament says that the word translated draw in John 6:44 means *"to compel by irresistible authority."* It was used in classical Greek for drawing water from a well. We do not entice or persuade water to leave the well; we force it against gravity to come up by drawing it. So it is with us. We are so depraved that God must drag us to himself." (Chosen by God)

The controversy is in whom God has chosen to be his sons and daughters. Hyper-Calvinists believe that some are chosen and some are not from the foundation of the world. Free Will folks, of which I am one, believe that what Jesus said, as recorded in John 3:16, qualifies all that accept his invitation. Listen to the verse and pay particular attention to the word, "WHOSOEVER" *"For God so loved the world that he gave his only begotten Son, that whosoever believeth in him should not perish, but have everlasting life."*

Jesus died for the sins of the whole world…every man, woman, boy and girl. The compelling call of God, through Jesus is an open invitation to whosoever will. These are the chosen of God that are pulled out of sin and given a new heart that can believe and worship him.

Now let's look again at how free will and sovereignty work hand and hand in our daily lives to fulfill God's master plan for the ages. Miles Monroe, a famous evangelist, once explained it this way…when God created the earth; He drew up a master plan, like an architect, that took into account every soul and every action that man would take. Nothing was left out.

God is never taken by surprise because he saw it before the world was. It was put into his plan. Then he began to create, taking into account who would accept Jesus and who would not; who would need deliverance; who would need help, etc. Every prayer and every need were seen beforehand. Your provision was made way back then and is waiting for the time you need it. You just have to grab it by faith.

This pre-design gives us free will to choose without violating God's Sovereignty. I know that some will say, I prayed and believed but didn't get what I asked for. My provision didn't materialize. It could be as James 4:3 says, *"Ye ask, and receive not, because ye ask amiss, that ye may consume it upon your lusts."* David Wilkerson, the author of The Cross & The Switchblade, offers six reasons that prayers go unanswered.

1. Our Prayers Are Aborted When They Are Not According To God's Will.
2. Our Prayers Can Be Aborted When They Are Designed To Fulfill An Inner Lust, Dreams, Or Illusions.
3. Our Prayers Can Be Denied When We Show No Diligence to Assist God In The Answer.
4. Our Prayers Can Be Aborted By A Secret Grudge Lodged In The Heart Against Another.
5. Our Prayers Can Be Aborted By Not Expecting Much To Come of Them.
6. Our Prayers Are Aborted When We Ourselves Attempt To Prescribe How God Should Answer. The devil's final strategy in deceiving believers is to make them doubt the faithfulness of God in answering prayer. Satan would have us believe God has shut his ears to our cry and left us to work things out for ourselves. That's just not true.

If you do not see the hand of God, you can bet that the problem is with you, not God. I'd suggest that you go back before the throne of God and stay there until you get an answer. Don't forget to take your Bible with you. *"Let us therefore come boldly unto the throne of grace that we may obtain mercy, and find grace to help in time of need."* (Hebrews 4:16)

One final thought. You may not be hearing the Lord because you are not "Born Again." Listen to what Jesus said, John 10:26-27, *"but you do not believe because you are not part of my flock. My sheep hear my voice, and I know them, and they follow me."*

If you are not hearing his voice, well, what should I say? You are not of his flock? Only you can determine that. It's a total life-changing commitment to follow Jesus. Maybe you did not make that kind of commitment. **He must be Lord of all or he is not Lord at all.**

The next time you make a decision, ask the Lord to show you if your decision is his will. If you have peace about what you are about to do, chances are it is God's will.

If you want to be happy, do so. It is up to you. If everything gets in your way, tell it to go away and laugh at it as though it were a bad joke. Go back to the scripture, Romans 8:28 and read it and believe it. God loves you and is for you and does not cause bad things to happen to you. They come from other sources. Romans 8:28 proves God's love because he steps in and works it out for your good.

CHAPTER THREE:
HAPPINESS BY RELATIONSHIP

Happiness is often a product of who you really are. That's why change is necessary. The biggest change is being "Born Again." It is the foundation from which all of life grows. Without it, you cannot hear the voice of God, or participate in his kingdom. You must be his child before you get his blessings. You will never know the Lord if you reject his salvation. So, let's look at being, "Born Again"

I have talked about being Born Again in almost every chapter. I did that so you would get use to the need and understand why. The following paragraphs are statistics from previous PEW reports. PEW is a very well-known resource for the study of trends and shifts in popular opinion like political, religious, and many more. According to PEW...

In 1965 — an astounding 93 percent of the United States population identified themselves as Christian. But again, the sixties were hardly representative of a "Christian" nation.

The point is that while the percentage of Christians in America was near its highest — the moral state of our society was far from "Christian. "In many ways, today's America is more Christian than at any previous moment in its history! Slavery and segregation have been abolished, gender inequality is on the decline, the wage gap has decreased, church communities are more diverse than ever, and people's rights and opportunities related to education, jobs, and opportunities are better than ever.

Today, Christians are more likely to consider themselves "born-again" or evangelical. Half of self-identified Christians described themselves this way in 2014, up from 44 percent in 2007.

Christianity is the most adhered religion in the United States, with 70.6% of polled American adults identifying themselves as Christian in 2014. This is down from 86% in 1990. (62% of those polled claim to be members of a church congregation.)

It should be noted that some folks that claim Christianity may very well be Born of the Spirit but are not familiar with the term, "Born Again." We do not want to pre-judge any one group. Statistics are just that, a snapshot in time. Data can be misleading and should be looked at as a guideline only.

The United States has the largest Christian population in the world, with nearly 247 million Christians, although other countries have higher percentages of Christians among their populations.

We have looked at Christianity as a religion. It is the only way that we can analyze it. However, the truth be known, being a Christian originally meant that you were a follower of Jesus, a disciple. It was not a religion but rather a relationship. A convert to Christianity went through a time of repentance, a plea for forgiveness, and an acceptance of Jesus as Lord.

Today, many churches offer a membership and boldly state that you can come just as you are, with no repentant heart, no plea for forgiveness and no need to live under the Lordship of Christ. **Here's what Jesus said**.

1. *"If any man come to me, and hate not his father, and mother, and wife, and children, and brethren, and sisters, yea, and his own life also, he cannot be my disciple."* **Luke 14:6**

The Contemporary English Version translates this verse like this, *"You cannot be my disciple, unless you love me more than you love your father and mother, your wife and children, and your brothers and sisters. You cannot come with me unless you love me more than you love your own life."* **Luke 14:6**

2. *"And when he had called the people to him with his disciples also, he said to them, whoever will come after me, let him deny himself, and take up his cross, and follow me. For whoever will save his life shall lose it; but whoever shall lose his life for My sake and the gospel's, the same shall save it."* **(Mar 8:34-35)**

3. *"Jesus answered and said unto him, Verily, verily, I say unto thee, except a man be born again, he cannot see the kingdom of God."* **John 3:3**

The Pew report tells us that there are a large percentage of evangelicals that do not identify themselves as, "Born Again." What happens to these folks?

Is there a different place that they will go when they die? According to Jesus, to see the kingdom of God, **you must be born again**. We know from the rest of the scriptures that there is a heaven, kingdom of God, and there is a Hell, a place of torment. It's either heaven or hell. Some will benefit and some will not.

Could it be that 51% of all Methodists, 55% of all Presbyterians, 63% of all Lutherans, 29% of all Adventists and 29% of all Restorationists will not see the kingdom of God?

The Pew report also says that 15 % of all Evangelicals and 21% of all non-denominational Christians do not identify themselves as, "Born Again" This report also says that 78% of all Catholics do not identify themselves as being, "Born Again".

The question is, are non "Born Again" Christians really children of God? I think it is important to examine why Jesus said, "You Must Be "Born Again." He was talking to Nicodemus, a ruler of the Jews of that day. Listen to the story as recorded by John, the apostle.

There was a man of the Pharisees named Nicodemus, a ruler of the Jews. This man came to Jesus by night and said to him, "Rabbi, we know that You are a teacher come from God; for no one can do these signs that You do unless God is with him." Jesus answered and said to him, "Most assuredly, I say to you, unless one is born again, he cannot see the kingdom of God."

Nicodemus said to him, ***"How can a man be born when he is old?*** Can he enter a second time into his mother's womb and be born?" Jesus answered, "Most assuredly, I say to you, unless one is born of water and the Spirit, he cannot enter the kingdom of God. That which is born of the flesh is flesh, and that which is born of the Spirit is spirit.

Do not marvel that I said to you, 'You must be born again.' The wind blows where it wishes, and you hear the sound of it, but cannot tell where it comes from and where it goes. So is everyone who is born of the Spirit." Nicodemus answered and said to him, "How can these things be?"

Jesus answered and said to him, "Are you the teacher of Israel, and do not know these things? Most assuredly, I say to you, we speak what we know and testify what we have seen, and you do not receive our witness. If I have told you earthly things and you do not believe, how will you believe if I tell you heavenly things?

No one has ascended to heaven but He who came down from heaven, *that is,* the Son of Man who is in heaven. And as Moses lifted up the serpent in the wilderness, even so must the Son of Man be lifted up, that whoever believes in Him should not perish but[b] have eternal life.

For God so loved the world that He gave His only begotten Son, that whoever believes in Him should not perish but have everlasting life. For God did not send His Son into the world to condemn the world, but that the world through Him might be saved. **John 3:1-16**

Nicodemus was a ruler of the Jews. That would be the equivalent to being a Pastor or Bible Teacher today. He was a member of an established religious group. He was seen as a man of authority, wisdom and one who was educated in the things of God. However, like many religious leaders of our day, he lacked the simple truth that makes a person a child of God.

It's not religion, being nice, doing good works, being smart, and wealthy or any earthly thing. Jesus qualified it by saying **you need a second birth, that of the Spirit to see and enter his kingdom**. This can only happen by believing in Jesus who is the only begotten Son of God. The first birth is not eternal due to sin but the second is eternal because of Christ. (See Romans Chapter 5)

DECEPTION RULES THE DAY

Sixty-five percent of all Christians say there are multiple paths to eternal life, ultimately rejecting the exclusivity of Christ teaching, according to the latest survey conducted by the Pew Forum on Religion and Public Life.

Even among white evangelical Protestants, 72 percent of those who say many religions can lead to eternal life name at least one non-Christian religion, such as Islam or no religion at all, that can lead to salvation.

Surprisingly, Christians also believe atheism can provide a ticket to heaven. Forty-six percent of white mainline Christians, 49 percent of white Catholics and 26 percent of white evangelicals who believe many religions lead to salvation say atheism can lead to eternal life.

THE BIBLE TELLS THE TRUTH

All of these folks that view the path to heaven as wide go against Biblical truth. Here's what the bible says:

1. *Neither is there salvation in any other: for there is none other name under heaven given among men, whereby we must be saved.* **Acts 4:12**
2. *Jesus saith unto him, I am the way, the truth, and the life: no man cometh unto the Father, but by me.* **John 14:6**
3. *I am the door: by me if any man enters in, he shall be saved, and shall go in and out, and find pasture.* **John 10:9**
4. *Behold, I stand at the door, and knock: if any man hear my voice, and open the door, I will come in to him, and will sup with him, and he with me.* **Revelation 3:20**

Jesus said, *"Enter ye in at the strait gate: for wide is the gate, and broad is the way, that leadeth to destruction, and many there be which go in thereat: Because strait is the gate, and narrow is the way, which leadeth unto life, and few there be that find it.* **Matthew 7:13-14**

It hurts me to read about how many people that claim to be Christian are deceived and on the wrong path in life. I guess they believe that their church will save them or their good works or the fact that they are worthy in some other way to qualify for eternal life.

Before we deal with how to be born again…to experience a new or second birth, it is important to look at why it is necessary and why Jesus is the only one that can get us to heaven.

JUST "ONE WAY?"

It is hard for most folks that are not "Born Again" to understand why there is just one way to God, yet it is true. There is only one way and that is through Jesus Christ. The Bible is our source to prove that the one-way doctrine is valid. **Acts 4:12** says, *"Neither is there salvation in any other: for there is none other name under heaven given among men, whereby we must be saved."*

Here's why it's so important. Adam sinned against God and died spiritually. *"And the LORD God commanded the man, saying, of every tree of the garden thou mayest freely eat: 17 But of the tree of the knowledge of good and evil, thou shalt not eat of it: for in the day that thou eat thereof thou shalt surely die."* **Genesis 2:16-17**

This creation account shows man being made of clay and God breathing into him the breath of life. He thus became a living soul. *"And the LORD God formed man of the dust of the ground, and breathed into his nostrils the breath of life; and man became a living soul."* **Genesis 2:7**. When he sinned, the breath of life was taken from him and he became a dead soul. He was truly the first of a race of the walking dead.

Life is always in relationship to God. It is his breath or Spirit that makes us alive. So, death passed upon all men for all sinned. **(Romans 5:12)** Their nature was now sinful. We see this in all of us and in our society. The second birth experience is by the Spirit. The Breath of Life is given to each repentant heart and their souls become alive to God. They become his children by birth. **Jesus is the only way to attain salvation.**

All the world religions cannot save us. Joining a church or specific faith cannot save us. It must be an acknowledgment of our sin, our cry before the throne of God for forgiveness, and our invitation for Jesus to come into our hearts and save us. His name is the only name that can get us through death into eternal life.

Here are a few scriptures that support the only "One-Way" doctrine.

1. *"there is one God, and one mediator between God and men, the man Christ Jesus; Who gave himself a ransom for all, to be testified in due time."* **(I Timothy 2:5-6)**
2. *"Believe on the Lord Jesus Christ and thou shalt be saved"* **(Acts 16:31)**
3. *"That if thou shalt confess with thy mouth the Lord Jesus, and shalt believe in thine heart that God hath raised him from the dead, THOU SHALT BE SAVED. For with the heart man be-*

lieveth unto righteousness; and with the mouth confession is made unto salvation." **(Romans 10:9-10)**

The skeptic would say, "You mean to tell me that all the religions of the world are wrong and only Christianity is the one true religion?" Remember, Christianity is not a religion. It is a relationship born out of love between man and the one true and living God. There is no one true religion. Religion, in itself, will not get us to God. It is the blood of Christ that unlocks the door and our confession of faith in Jesus that makes it all happen. **(John 14:6)**

Why is Jesus the only way to God? ...Because God planned it that way. He set the penalty for sin, which was death. *The soul that sinneth, it shall die.* **(Ezekiel 18:20)** In fact, Jesus was the slain Lamb of God before the foundation of the world. **(Ephesians 1:3-7)**

Jesus himself said, as recorded in **John 14:6**, *"I am the way, the truth, and the life: No man cometh to the Father but by me"*. Christianity states that the God of the Bible is the only true God and salvation is only possible by accepting Jesus Christ, his only begotten Son as Savior and Lord. **II Corinthians 5:21** says, *"For he hath made him to be sin for us, who knew no sin; that we might be made the righteousness of God in him."*

God validated his Son as the only way in multiple ways so we could be assured that Jesus was indeed the only way to him. Here are some to consider.

1. He claimed to be the only way as in John's record 14:6 says but validation came through miracles that proved he was who he claimed to be.
2. Eyewitnesses saw Jesus' miracles and validated them as authentic. Over 500 followers saw Jesus, after his resurrection, and watched him ascend into heaven.
3. The prophets foretold of his coming, where he would be born, that he would be God in human flesh and lots more...all pro-

phetic statements were realized in Jesus, even those like in Isaiah chapter 53 that were uttered hundreds of years before Jesus came.

4. God Himself validated Jesus as his sole pathway to him. *"While he was still speaking, behold, a bright cloud overshadowed them; and suddenly a voice came out of the cloud, saying, "This is My beloved Son, in whom I am well pleased. Hear ye Him!"* **(Mathew 17:5)**

5. The Apostles lost their homes, wealth, and even their lives preaching the gospel. Would they do that if it were a lie? I don't think so. They testified to the truth and were willing to die for it if necessary. (Check out Foxes Book of Martyrs)

6. Thousands of Believers, over several centuries have testified of how Jesus helped them and blessed them.

7. I can personally testify that I have seen the hand of the Lord in my life and communicate with him daily. I know he is the Christ. The provability that one man could fulfill all prophecies about a Messiah that God himself said would come, **(Gen.3:15)**, and perform fantastic miracles while here on earth, and be raised from the dead, and ascend into heaven while hundreds looked on is astronomical. But Jesus did just that…fulfilled everything that was foretold about the coming Messiah. He had to be who he said he was and therefore is truly the only way to God.

HOW TO BE BORN AGAIN

It should be obvious by now that it is essential for anyone who wants eternal life to be, "Born Again." **Romans 10:9-10** will tell us how. *"That if thou shalt confess with thy mouth the Lord Jesus, and shalt believe in thine heart that God hath raised him from the dead, thou shalt be saved. For with the heart man believeth unto righteousness; and with the mouth confession is made unto salvation."* **Romans 10:9-10**

Confessing Jesus is to acknowledge his Lordship and openly proclaim your allegiance. There is no secret society. That's why the scripture says, "With Thy Mouth." Believing with the heart is different than with the mind. When we believe

with our heart, it means to rely upon, adhere to and trust in. We are to wholly embrace the truth that God raised up Jesus from the dead after being crucified for the sins of mankind.

The power to save us and birth us into his kingdom as his child is in the fact that our heartfelt belief brings us the righteousness of Christ and our open mouth of continual confession in him as our savior actually saves us.

Remember what Paul wrote to the Romans. He said, in effect, that Adam was the 1st man who fell into sin and took the entire race with him. Thus, death passed upon all of us. However, Jesus was the second Adam or man that was sent outside of the pollution of human sinful DNA via a virgin birth to be the spotless Lamb of God and to be slain as a sacrifice for sin to abolish it forever. This is why the "New Birth" is necessary, to free us from the sin of the 1st Adam and propel us by spiritual birth into the Kingdom of God.

HOW DO WE KNOW FOR SURE THAT WE ARE, "BORN AGAIN?"

"The Spirit itself beareth witness with our spirit, that we are the children of God: And if children, then heirs; heirs of God, and joint-heirs with Christ; if so be that we suffer with him, that we may be also glorified together." **Romans 8:15-17**

We who have believed can say that we are his children, without a doubt or any question in our minds. We can because the Spirit of God is continually bearing witness with our spirits. He leads us; He communicates with us; He teaches us and shows us truth and error. **That's how we know for sure.** If you have never seen the hand of God in your life or heard the spirit speaking to you, you might want to go back to God and repent of your sins, ask his forgiveness and ask Jesus to come into your heart and save you. Then receive Jesus as your Lord and Savior. This is the only way you can be born again.

HOW DOES THIS "BORN AGAIN" EXPERIENCE CHANGE US

And you were dead in your trespasses and sins, in which you formerly walked according to the course of this world, according to the prince of the power of the air, of the spirit that is now working in the sons of disobedience. Among them we too all formerly lived in the lusts of our flesh, indulging the desires of the flesh and of the mind, and were by nature children of wrath, even as the rest. But God, being rich in mercy, because of his great love with which He loved us, even when we were dead in our transgressions, made us alive together with Christ (by grace you have been saved), and raised us up with him, and seated us with him in the heavenly places in Christ Jesus, so that in the ages to come he might show the surpassing riches of his grace in kindness toward us in Christ Jesus. for by grace.

You have been saved through faith; and that not of yourselves, it is the gift of God; not as a result of works, so that no one may boast. For we are his workmanship, created in Christ Jesus for good works, which God prepared beforehand so that we would walk in them. remember that you were at that time separate from Christ, excluded from the commonwealth of Israel, and strangers to the covenants of promise, having no hope and without God in the world. But now in Christ Jesus you who formerly were far off have been brought near by the blood of Christ. For he himself is our peace, who made both groups into one and broke down the barrier of the dividing wall, by abolishing in his flesh the enmity, which is the Law of commandments contained in ordinances, so that in himself

He might make the two into one new man, thus establishing peace, and might reconcile them both in one body to God through the cross, by it having put to death the enmity. AND HE CAME AND PREACHED PEACE TO YOU WHO WERE FAR AWAY, AND PEACE TO THOSE WHO WERE NEAR; *for through Him we both have our access in one Spirit to the Father.*

So then you are no longer strangers and aliens, but you are fellow citizens with the saints, and are of God's household, having been built on the foundation of the apostles and prophets, Christ Jesus Himself being the corner stone, in whom the whole building, being fitted together, is growing into a holy temple in the Lord, in whom you also are being built together into a dwelling of God in the Spirit. **Ephesians 2:1-22 ASV**

Read this again. It tells you where you were or are now and where God takes you when you are Born Again. It is truly a life changing experience.

BENEFITS OF BEING, "BORN AGAIN"

The above scripture passage reveals 10 benefits that overtake the believer at his new birth. They are:

1. We experience God's great Mercy and Love…verse #4
2. We are made alive to God, given eternal life…verse #5
3. We were raised up with Christ and seated with him in Heavenly
4. Places…. verse #6
5. We receive his Grace or unmerited favor…Verse # 8
6. We are brought close to God by the Blood of Christ…verse #13
7. Jesus becomes our peace…verse #14
8. We gain access to God through his Spirit…verse #18
9. We are no longer strangers but fellow citizens and joint heirs with Christ…verse 19

10. We are becoming a spiritual dwelling for God…verse #22
11. We are his workmanship, created in Christ Jesus unto good works that were established before we were saved so we could walk in them…v#10

We have looked at statistics that show trends and percentages of those in error. We have discussed doctrines like Jesus as the only pathway to God the Father. We have looked at benefits of being," Born Again," and why it is necessary to attain eternal life. We have seen how to be Born again through repentance, a plea for forgiveness and an invitation to Jesus to enter our hearts and be Lord over our lives. There is only one thing left to do, decide for yourself.

CHAPTER FOUR:
HAPPINESS THROUGH GOD'S HOLY SPIRIT

If you are experiencing joy, you are happy. No one can be sad or depressed and experience joy at the same time. The Bible says a lot about Joy and how it affects human beings.

The only true joy is found in God. It is listed among the fruit of the Spirit. We cannot muster it up within ourselves. It is only found in the Spiritual realm. Here's what the Bible says:

"But the **fruit of the Spirit** *is love, joy, peace, longsuffering, gentleness, goodness, faith, meekness, temperance: against such there is no law."* Galatians 5:22-23

Notice that Joy is listed among the different aspects of the fruit. That is because the word, "Fruit" is another word for Character. That's why fruit is used as a single item. Otherwise, it would say, fruits. The very character of God is Love, Joy, Peace, Longsuffering, and so on. (Galatians chapter five)

The great thing about the fruit of the Spirit is that he will share it with us. We can experience the character of God. He will fill us with himself. We need only to ask. I ask my heavenly Father every day to fill me with his Holy Spirit…and I know that he does. I can actually feel it in me.

Can you imagine actually walking in the love of God, being full of his joy, and experiencing his peace, that passes all understanding? Well, you don't have to imagine. It is real and you can have it even now. Just ask the Lord. *"he who comes to God must believe that He is, and that He is a rewarder of those who diligently seek Him."* Hebrews 11:6b

Let's look at some scripture about the Joy of the Lord. Joy brings happiness.

"Do not grieve, for the joy of the LORD is your strength." **Nehemiah 8:10** God is a happy God. He loves us and wants the best for us at all times. His joy can and often does become a source of strength in times of trouble.

"But let all those that put their trust in thee rejoice: let them ever shout for joy, because thou defendest them: let them also that love thy name be joyful in thee." Psalm 5:11 There is good reason to be happy.

"My Brethren, count it all joy when you fall in to diverse temptations, knowing this, that the trying of your faith worketh patience." **James 1:2-3** There is always a reason for that. God allows us to experience difficulties so we learn patience. This brings about longsuffering which is a Godly attribute.

"Hitherto have ye asked nothing in my name: ask, and ye shall receive, that your joy may be full." **John 16:24** If we ask the Lord for those things that will make us happy, he will provide them. Of course, it must be in accordance to his will. He will not give us stuff to consume or fulfill our own lust.

"A merry heart does good like a medicine: but a broken spirit dries the bones." **Proverbs 17:22 Good health starts with being happy. Doing the will of God, knowing that his destiny for us is good, will cause us to have a merry heart and keep us healthy.**

"For the kingdom of God is not meat and drink; but righteousness, and peace, and joy in the Holy Ghost." **Romans 14:17** When we have the Joy of the Lord, we arrive at true happiness. Guess what? That can only be attained by receiving the Holy Ghost. He brings the kingdom of God here on earth as it is in heaven and displays it in and through us.

"This is the day which the LORD hath made; we will rejoice and be glad in it." **Psalms 118:24** Joy or happiness is a choice. Because God made the day, we shall rejoice or be happy in it. No matter what is going on around us, we must decide to be happy. We do this by knowing that God will work everything out for good. **(Romans 8:28)** and that he will never leave us or forsake us. **(Hebrews 13:5)**

"The hope of the righteous will be gladness, but the expectation of the wicked will perish." **Proverbs 10:28** Our hope is gladness. We rejoice at the thought of God's love and provisions.

"Go, eat your bread with joy, and drink your wine with a merry heart; for God has already accepted your works." **Ecclesiastes 9:7 Being accepted by God is the key to being happy in this life. That comes only through his Son, Jesus Christ. Acts 4:12**

There are many other scriptures that talk about joy, rejoicing, happy and so on. I have sampled a few so you get the point. It all boils down to individual choice. The Spirit of God will give us divine revelation as to what choice is best but he does not force it upon us.

We must accept what he says and apply it to our lives. It is for sure a cooperative partnership between man and God. He wants us to participate in shaping our own destiny and will always point to the right path to walk. Hear what the Bible says about that. *"And thine ears shall hear a word behind thee, saying, this is the way, walk ye in it"* **Isiah 30:21**

Have you ever heard the voice of God?.... People tell me that I am crazy because I say, "God told me", Or "the Spirit of the Lord led me to this decision." They think I am crazy. Guess what" I am not crazy. I hear the voice of the Lord every day. He invades my thoughts with scripture, Bible truths, direction in life and many other situational questions and answers.

Hear again what Jesus said, *"My sheep hear my voice, and I know them, and they follow me: And I give unto them eternal life; and they shall never perish, neither shall any man pluck them out of my hand."* **John 10:27-28**

We are commanded to walk in the Spirit of God. The purpose of this command is so we will not fulfill the lust of the flesh. Listen to what the apostle Paul said to the 1st century Christians.

"This I say then, *walk in the Spirit, and ye shall not fulfill the lust of the flesh"* **(Galatians 5:16).** Then again, *"if we live in the Spirit, let us also walk in the Spirit"* **(Galatians 5:25).**

Although they appear to be the same command in English, there is a significant distinction in the original Greek language in which Paul penned the letters.

Both the **Romans 8:1** and the **Galatians 5:16** passages use the word *perepeto*, which carries the connotation to "walk around" and to "be at liberty."

The second iteration in **Galatians 5:25** uses *stoicheo*, which means to "step precisely," to "march," or to "go in procession." Same command but different emphasis. (Excerpts from an article by Henry M. Morris III, D. Min. Institute for Creation Research)

The use of two different words tells me that we have liberty to hang around with God in his Spirit to fellowship with him but we also must walk precisely along the path he has shown us to achieve victory.

As a young Christian, I often wondered what it meant to actually walk in God's Holy Spirit. I was also curious to know how to live in the Spirit. Was there a set of rules? How does one live and walk in the Spirit of the Living God? Is it actually possible? As I grew in Bible knowledge, it all became clear to me. I do have to admit that it is still hard some times to stay in the Spirit and even walk in him because the devil is hard after me to walk in the flesh. I falter now and then but no one is perfect.

Galatians 5 offers a contrast between a lifestyle of fleshly behavior and a life controlled by the Holy Spirit. The "deeds" of the flesh and the "fruit" of the Spirit are diametrically opposed. They continually fight for control of our minds so as to manifest their image here on the earth through us. However, they cannot exist together; they are not co-rulers. (Romans 8:5-8) We either "mind" the things of the flesh or the "things of the Spirit." (Romans 8:5)

ONLY, "BORN AGAIN" FOLKS CAN WALK IN THE SPIRIT

I'll bet you didn't know that you cannot be or live in neutrality. We are created beings by God for one primary purpose...to reveal his image upon the earth. The original plan was that mankind would live and walk in the Spirit on this earth as a reflection of God. To see us would be like seeing God because we looked just like him. *"So God created man in his own image, in the image of God created he him; male and female created he them."* **Genesis 1:27**

However, sin entered the world and replaced the image of God with the image of Satan. **(Romans 5:12)** Mankind now is ruled by evil instead of good. His nature and character reveal the sin that reigns in his heart. He has no choice but to live out this evil destiny.

All that God wanted for mankind was lost because he no longer dwelt in the Spirit of God. Even his love became distorted and his whole reasoning fell into a selfish gratification. God's race of Godly children, fashioned in his own likeness, was lost, seemingly forever. Man became a distortion of mind and body that led to a worldwide flood, a sentence of death for all who are called human after Adam's kind. *"For all have sinned, and come short of the glory of God"* **Romans 3:23**

GOD'S PLAN OF REDEMPTION

But God did not leave man in such a depraved state with no choice. He honored his own plan for the ages which was to allow man to have a, "Free Will" and to be his own free moral agent. His Lordship over man would not be evil but righteous as he restored man to a status of being able, once again, to walk in his Spirit. The choice was given back to man. He can now choose to live in sin or walk in the righteousness of God.

We also know that it was God that designed this plan of redemption and set it in motion, even before the foundation of the world. That plan was Christ crucified, once for all, that whosoever believes in him, this Jesus of Nazareth, who died as a penalty for sin, who was made sin for us, would not perish but have everlasting life. **(Ephesians 1:4, John 3:16, II Corinthians 5:21)**

So, only those that accept God's plan of salvation have the choice of walking in his Spirit. Those that do not believe and do not accept the free gift of salvation through faith are bound by their own evil nature to live out a destiny that is the image and likeness of Satan.

TWO NATURES ONE CHOICE

"For the flesh lusts against the Spirit, and the Spirit against the flesh: and these are contrary the one to the other: so that ye cannot do the things that ye would." **(Galatians 5:17)** We, that is, us Christians, are constantly being offered a choice. We can select the fruit of God's Spirit or the Works of the Flesh.

Galatians 5:22 describes the fruit and the works. *"But the fruit of the Spirit is love, joy, peace, longsuffering, gentleness, goodness, faith, Meekness, temperance: against such there is no law."*

Galatians 5:19-21 tells us what the works of the flesh are, *"Now the works of the flesh are manifest, which are these; Adultery, fornication, uncleanness, lasciviousness, Idolatry, witchcraft, hatred, variance, emulations, wrath, strife, seditions, heresies, envying, murders, drunkenness, reviling, and such like: of the which I tell you before, as I have also told you in time past, that they which do such things shall not inherit the kingdom of God.*

Now here's the kicker*…"And they that are Christ's have crucified the flesh with the affections and lusts."* **Galatians 5:24**

We crucify the flesh by denying it access to our emotions. We put it to death by not allowing it to be manifested in us. We will still get angry but we do not allow that anger to be released. Instead, we focus on the fruit of God's Spirit to overcome the flesh, thus filling ourselves with the image and likeness of God. Instead of getting angry, we pray for and demonstrate longsuffering and love. This is not easy to do. It will take practice and dedication to the word of God. Good luck!

The phrase "walk in the Spirit" occurs not only in Galatians 5:25 but also in verse 16, *"But I say, walk in the Spirit and do not gratify the desires of the flesh."* So here we see what the opposite of walking by the Spirit is, namely, giving in to the desires of the flesh.

Remember, "flesh" is the ordinary human nature that does not relish the things of God and prefers to get satisfaction from a sinful lifestyle. When we "walk in the Spirit," we are not controlled by those things. This is what verse 17 means: the flesh produces one kind of desire, and the Spirit produces another and they are opposed or contrary to each other.

Paul said in **Romans 7:18**, *"I know that in me, that is, in my flesh, dwells no good thing."* He also said *"for the mind of the flesh is hostile to God's law and does not submit to it because it cannot."* **(Romans 8:7)**

The new birth creates a whole new array of desires that want to please God. Therefore, "walking in the Spirit" is something the Holy Spirit enables us to do by producing in us strong desires that are in accord with God's will. This is what God said he would do in **Ezekiel 36:26, 27:** *"A new heart I will give you and a new spirit I will put within you . . . I will put my Spirit within you and cause you to walk in my statutes."*

Thus, when we *"walk in the Spirit,"* we can and do experience the fulfillment of this prophecy.

THE BIG QUESTION

This brings up a big question in my mind that you too may be asking… Do I just sit back and wait for new desires before I can walk in the Spirit? Of course not!

"And be not drunk with wine, wherein is excess; but be filled with the Spirit; Speaking to yourselves in psalms and hymns and spiritual songs, singing and making melody in your heart to the Lord; Giving thanks always for all things unto God and the Father in the name of our Lord Jesus Christ" **Ephesians 5:18-20**

There are several things we need to do in order to establish and continue our walk in the Spirit. I offer these as a starting point for your consideration:

1. **Pray to be filled with the Spirit…** *"And be not drunk with wine, wherein is excess; but be filled with the Spirit."* **Ephesians 5:18**

Then do what Ephesians says…The more we sing, make melody, read psalms and pray, the longer we stay filled. When our thoughts are on the things of the Lord, they cannot be dwelling on the things of the flesh. Some folks refer to this action as "Practicing the Presence of God."

2. **Have no confidence in the flesh…** *"For we are the circumcision, which worship God in the spirit, and rejoice in Christ Jesus, and have no confidence in the flesh. Though I might also*

have confidence in the flesh" **Philippians 3:3** (The Flesh is the unregenerate man that is led by Satan via a nature of sin)

When we have no confidence in the flesh, we do not put any faith in our own decision-making power. We always consult the Lord about what to do in any given situation. *We do not rely on our emotions.*

3. **Resist The devil and he will flee from you**...*Be sober, be vigilant; because your adversary the devil, as a roaring lion, walketh about, seeking whom he may devour:* **I Peter 5:8-9**

When we resist the devil, we are resisting his invitations to operate independently from God. He wants us to live in the flesh because it is his nature and if we do so, will manifest the image and likeness of Satan, the evil one. *Thus, the purpose of his temptations is to keep us from walking in the Spirit.*

4. **Walk By Faith:** *"For we walk by faith, not by sight"* **(II Corinthians 5:7)**

When we walk by faith, we walk in the promises of God that are given to us in the Bible. We actually live in them. If God said it, we will believe it and apply it in our lives. We will hold on to every word, knowing that God will cause every promise he has spoken into our spirits to come true. This keeps us free from any and all distraction that would lead us away from walking in the Spirit.

SPIRITUAL BREATHING
By Bill Bright off Campus Crusade

The Christian life, properly understood, is not complex nor is it difficult. As a matter of fact, the Christian life is very simple. It is so simple that we stumble over the very simplicity of it, and yet it is so difficult that no one can live it!

This paradox occurs because the Christian life is a supernatural life. The only one who can help us live this abundant life is the Lord Jesus Christ who empowers us with His Holy Spirit.

One of the most important truths of Scripture, the understanding and application of which has enriched my life as has no other truth, is a concept which I like to call *"Spiritual Breathing."* This concept has been shared with millions – with revolutionary results – through our literature and various training conferences and seminars.

As you walk in the Spirit by faith, practicing Spiritual Breathing, you need never again live in spiritual defeat. Spiritual Breathing, like physical breathing, is a process of exhaling the impure and inhaling the pure, an exercise in faith that enables you to experience God's love and forgiveness and walk in the Spirit as a way of life. (*You breath in the Word of God and you exhale the negative destructive emotions*)

The moment you invited Christ into your life as Savior and Lord, you experienced a spiritual birth. You became a child of God and you were filled with the Holy Spirit. God forgave your sins – past, present and future – making you righteous, holy and acceptable in his sight because of Christ's sacrifice for you on the cross. You were given the power to live a holy life and to be a fruitful witness for God.

But the average Christian does not understand this concept of Spiritual Breathing as an exercise of faith and, as a result, lives on a spiritual roller coaster. He goes from one emotional experience to another living most of his life as a worldly Christian, controlling his own life – frustrated and fruitless.

If this is your experience, Spiritual Breathing will enable you to get off this emotional rollercoaster and enjoy the Christian life that the Lord Jesus promised to you when He said, *"I came that they might have life and might have it abundantly."* **John 10:10**

As an exercise in faith, Spiritual Breathing will make it possible for you to continue to experience God's love, forgiveness, and the power of the Holy Spirit as a way of life.

If you try to live the Christian life by your own fleshly effort, it becomes complex, difficult and even impossible. But when you invite the Lord Jesus to direct your life; when you know the reality of having been crucified with Christ and raised with him by faith as a way of life; when you walk in the light as God is in the light in the fullness and power of the Holy Spirit, the Lord Jesus simply lives his abundant life within you in all of his resurrection power.

I'm not suggesting that the Christian who walks in the fullness of the Spirit will have no difficulties. Problems of poor health, loss of loved ones, financial needs and other such experiences are common to all people. However, many of our misfortunes are self-imposed because of our own worldly, selfish actions.

The spiritual person is spared most of these self-imposed hardships. But when the problems do come, the spiritual person can face them with a calm, confident attitude because he is aware of God's resources, which are available to him to deal with adversity. (Excerpts from Bill Bright's article from The Power to Change)

BEING CONTINUALLY FILLED

The command of **Ephesians 5:18** is given to all believers to be filled, directed and empowered by the Holy Spirit. Being filled with the Holy Spirit, however, is a continuous experience. In the Greek language in which this command was originally written, the meaning is clearer than that in most English translations. This command of God means to *be constantly and continually filled*, controlled and empowered by the Holy Spirit as a way of life.

If you look at the scripture from verse 15-18 you see a truth that few have really understood. See if you see what I see.

"See then that ye walk circumspectly, not as fools, but as wise, redeeming the time, because the days are evil. Wherefore be ye not unwise, but understanding what the will of the Lord is. And be not drunk with wine, wherein is excess; but be filled with the Spirit; [19] *Speaking to yourselves in psalms and hymns and spiritual songs, singing and making melody in your heart to the Lord;* [20] *Giving thanks always for all things unto God and the Father in the name of our Lord Jesus Christ."* **Galatians 5:15-20**

Here's what I see:

1. We are to use wisdom and not to be as fools. In doing so, we can redeem the time lost to the past in living in sin.
2. We are not to drink in excess but in contrast to that life style, we are to be continually filled with God's Spirit. This is the will of the Lord.
3. The way we keep ourselves filled with the Spirit is to sing, make melody in our hearts and give thanks to our Heavenly Father in the name of Jesus.

The process of praise, prayer and reading the psalms will keep you from the flesh and drunkenness. It will also continually fill you with the Spirit. We receive faith by reading the Word. We are filled with Joy by singing. We are blessed with peace by giving thanks. It all comes together inside of us to continually keep us in the Spirit.

Note: Some have said that we leak and the spirit, like water, drains out of us. This is nothing more than foolishness. We are faced with a choice in life, to dwell in the flesh and to ride the emotional rollercoaster or to be filled with the Spirit and walk in peace with God through this upside-down world.

We can, however, fall back into the flesh. Paul wrote to the Galatians and said, *"O foolish Galatians, who hath bewitched you, that ye should not obey the truth, before whose eyes Jesus Christ hath been evidently set forth, crucified among you? ² This only would I learn of you, Received ye the Spirit by the works of the law, or by the hearing of faith? ³ Are ye so foolish having begun in the Spirit, are ye now made perfect by the flesh?"* **Galatians 3:1-3**

The Galatians started out in the Spirit but somehow believed a lie and went back into the works of the law, which opposed the grace of God. Paul called them foolish. This example shows how the devil can lead you away from the truth and cause you to operate in the flesh. That's how he defeats Christians. He spins a lie and we get confused and end up believing it and eventually it changes our thinking.

Remember, non-believers do not have two natures. They can only operate in the flesh. Seeing the state of our current society with so much evil, the flesh is running rampant.

However, we are blessed with a new nature that is holy and righteous in every way. It is the same nature of Jesus and the very likeness of God. It is his image. We can choose the new and reject the old and walk in his Spirit. This is a benefit of the New Birth experience when we are "Born Again."

When we strive to walk with God and fellowship with him, we are always attacked by the devil because the devil does not want us doing that. He wants us in the flesh so he can torment us. However, he cannot even get to us when we are "In the Spirit." He has to draw us away with some sort of temptation or lie. *"But every man is tempted, when he is drawn away of his own lust, and enticed. Then when lust hath conceived, it bringeth forth sin: and sin, when it is finished, bringeth forth death"* James 1:14-15

Many Christians avoid the Spirit. There are many reasons why. Let's look at a few.

1. **FEAR OF REJECTION**..."*But God forbid that I should glory, save in the cross of our Lord Jesus Christ, by whom the world is crucified unto me, and I unto the world.*" **Gal. 6:14**

In the above scripture we can see that the cross is the *mark of distinction* between the world and us. Sometimes I hear people say, "I want to walk with God but I don't know how I could ever give up my friends." My answer to that is very simple: If you begin to walk with the Lord, you won't have to worry about giving up your friends; you won't have time for that--they will give you up first. That is how the cross is a mark of distinction.

2. **LIVING BY YOUR FEELINGS AND NOT BY FAITH**... As we have already said, living in the flesh is living by your feelings. It offers only a terrifying ride on that emotional rollercoaster.

3. **FAILURE IN SIMPLE OBEDIENCE**...Again we look to Galatians where Paul tells the church, "Ye did run well; who did hinder you that ye should not obey the truth?" Disobedience will always stop the flow of God's anointing and kick us out of his Spirit. There is nowhere to go but back into the flesh.

4. **ALLOWING OTHERS TO HINDER YOU**...Again in Galatians, it was someone or many that hindered the church from obeying the truth. We cannot allow others to sway us from the truth.

5. **GIVING IN TO TEMPTATION**...Temptation will do it every time. It will cause you to fall if you give into to it. Paul, in **Galatians 3:1** said, *"Oh foolish Galatians"* He knew that they had given into the pressures and expectations of others. Their desire to be politically correct was stronger than their desire to obey the truth. We can never give in.

SEEING WHAT'S NOT VISIBLE

As I mentioned before, the Christian has two natures and must choose one or the other. Both natures will calamor for attention and the chance for expression. One is Holy and the other is Evil.

The evil nature has polluted our souls, invaded our DNA and dominated our emotions. Its rule over us is cruel. Its goal is to manifest wickedness as a lifestyle.

The holy nature is newly fashioned as a "Born Again" experience where we repented of our sin and put our faith in Jesus. Its goal is to manifest the fruit of God's Spirit through a gentle Lordship where we can be blessed and live an abundant life.

Because we have the dominant nature of evil inside of us, we see life through its eyes and process events on an emotional level. The new nature of holiness is equally capable of sight but looks only into the spirit realm. It sees and discerns spiritual things. It processes events based upon the Will of God and the believer's divine destiny.

The holy nature in you relies on divine revelation from its creator. The result is divine wisdom that enhances our ability to make Godly decisions. You cannot walk in the Spirit without seeing in the Spirit. *The eyes of the Spirit are the scriptures.* It is there that our eyes are opened and our focus made clear.

Now that you kind of know about how the two natures operate in us when called upon, it is important to realize that there is another, "Free Will" choice to be made…which nature to call upon. We are bent on the evil nature. Holiness is contrary to our natural feel. To allow it to advise and control our decisions is not automatic. That's why we are encouraged to deny the flesh by crucifying it with all its lust and evil affections. We have to deny the evil in order to live in the Holy nature.

When we are faced with a situation or happening, we automatically make a decision on what to do. As a man, I am often confronted with women crossing my path or coming into my line of sight. If my human nature is ruling, my emotions will spike and I will most likely fall into some sort of fantasy. If, on the other hand, my holy nature is in control, I automatically hear the scriptures speaking in my head telling me what the Word of God says about the situation and what I need to do to stay in the Spirit.

If you do not know the scriptures, you will walk as a blind man and be unable to discern the times you live in. The snares of the devil, the demonic temptations and fiery darts, will be hurled at you and the many day- to- day decisions will overwhelm you.

The psalmist said, *"Thy word have I hid in mine heart, that I might not sin against thee."* **Psalm 119:11** Without the hiding of God's Word in your heart, you have nothing to draw from to make a holy decision. You are blind and could easily fall back into the human nature that once ruled your life and wrecked your emotions.

The Christian walk has great liberty **(Romans 8:21),** but that liberty must "step precisely" in honesty **(Romans 13:13)**, good works **(Ephesians 2:10),** and in truth **(2 John 4-6).**

Our walk is expected to be by faith and not by sight (2 **Corinthians 5:7)** We are to conduct spiritual warfare in the Holy Spirit's power **(2 Corinthians 10:3-5)** We are to protect ourselves by putting on the full armor of God **(Ephesians 6:10-18).**

However, the most important thing to remember is that we need to stay in the Spirit and we can only do that by reading the scriptures to gain faith, singing and making melody in our hearts unto the Lord and giving thanks to our heavenly Father in the name of Jesus. *That is what keeps us in the Spirit and ultimately happy.*

I will caution all that read this book. It is not advisable to move back and forth from one nature to the other because it creates an emotional rollercoaster that will drive you crazy and keep you from your divine destiny.

May our Lord bless you as you walk with him. If you are not a believer, stay tuned. We will be discussing the, "Born Again" experience in more detail.

CHAPTER FIVE:
HAPPINESS AND PERSECUTION

If you cannot be happy in the midst of adversity, it's probably because you have an adversary that wants to kill, steal and destroy your life. Most Christians give up and fall prey to those evil forces that lurk in the shadows.

I guess they forgot the one part of the Lord's prayer that says, *"Thou preparest a table before me in the presence of mine enemies."* Adversity and evil purposed people are part of life. They are all around us. However, true happiness is to sit down at the table set just for you and enjoy the banquet, even though you are surrounded by your enemies.

I'll bet you did not know that you have an unseen evil enemy that lurks around every situation seeking to destroy your very soul? Jesus said, as recorded in John 10:10, *"The thief does not come except to steal, and to kill, and to destroy. I have come that they may have life, and that they may have it more abundantly."*

Peter said, *"Be sober, be vigilant; because your adversary the devil walks about like a roaring lion, seeking whom he may devour."* I Peter 5:8

Sadly enough, 40% of professing Christians do not believe in Satan as a real being. The majority of American Christians do not believe that Satan is a real being or that the Holy Spirit is a living entity, according to the latest George Barna survey.

Nearly **six out of ten** Christians surveyed either strongly agreed or somewhat agreed with the statement that Satan "is not a living being but is a symbol of evil." The same survey indicated that only 35% of those surveyed believe in God.

I am here to tell you that Satan is a real being and he is after you, to steel, kill and destroy your soul. If he can influence you on a soulish level, he can capture you and use you as his tool to hurt others.

It all happens in the mind, will and emotions, (The Soul), before it plays out in reality. A good example is how he can spin a lie and kill more than 60 million babies. He just said that abortion is a matter of women's health and they should make the life-or-death choice. They believe that it is not the mother's sin that murders innocent babies in the womb. It's just a good health choice.

Did you know that there is a heartbeat within 13-19-day of conception? Yet in many states legal abortions can take place even in the last trimester, at full term.

This unseen enemy is none other than Satan. He is the *Enemy of Your Soul*. He is also known as the devil, the evil one, the wicked one, the god of this world, the ruler of darkness and the father of lies. He is after you and every other human being.

He, as Peter said, roams the earth, like a roaring lion, seeking whom he may devour. However, He is a defeated foe but yet very powerful. The sure way to win over such an evil force is to resist him steadfastly in the faith as I Peter 5:9 says. *"Whom resist steadfast in the faith, knowing that the same afflictions are accomplished in your brethren that are in the world."*

Jesus defeated Satan at the cross over 2,000 years ago. Satan has no power but what he can steal from you. He wants to establish strongholds in your life, through which he can control your emotions and manipulate your actions.

These strongholds are in your mind. It is how you think about things, your perspective in life. If he can alter the way you think, he can slowly but surely control you and ultimately establish a stronghold.

Before demonic strongholds can be overcome, we should understand exactly what they are. The word stronghold appears only once in the New Testament (2 Corinthians 10:4), and the Greek word translated "stronghold" means "a fortification such as a castle." In this passage, the apostle Paul is instructing the church at Corinth on how to fight against and "destroy arguments and every lofty opinion raised against the knowledge of God" (2 Corinthians 10:5). They do this, not by using the weapons of the world, but by "divine power."

Lofty arguments and opinions are the result of pride and evil and vain imaginations, the very strongholds in which demons reside. This, then, is the essence of demonic warfare—the power of God to overcome the dwelling place of demons.

Practical Application of II Corinthians 10:5

We can use this scripture as a pathway to victory over evil, no matter where it comes from. The key is to bring every thought into the light of the Word of God. Then cast down or reject every thought that sets itself above the Knowledge of God.

You can hold the thought captive and judge it by what you know is true from the scripture. This keeps you from acting upon thoughts that do not agree with God's Word/Will. We can put our thoughts and what others tell us on trial.

A good example of this technique played out in action is a thought entering your mind that you can steal from your neighbor who is on vacation. No one will ever know. The victory is seen in holding that thought captive to the scripture in the 10-commandmeents that say, "Thou shalt not steal" Now that you know stealing is not God's will, you dismiss the thought and send it on its way, giving it no expression in your reality.

AGENTS OF TORMENT

We have already learned that the devil is the source of evil. His demons are hard at work to kill, steal and destroy. What may not be apparent is whom these evil forces work through. Here's a short list, this time of the "Agents of Terror."

Consider these folks; Mom, Dad, Siblings, Teachers, Co-Workers, Other Christians, Religious Leaders and so on. Anyone that allows access to evil thoughts can become an agent of torment and oppression.

The apostle Paul wrote this to the first century church, *"For we wrestle not against flesh and blood, but against principalities, against powers, against the rulers of the darkness of this world, against spiritual wickedness in high places."* **Ephesians 6:12**

Yes, almost anyone can be used by evil forces to oppose us but our battle is not with them. They are only pawns in the hands of the devil. They might even think they are doing a good thing. It will be obvious to us that they have no Spiritual insight.

So, what do we do with the flesh and bones that come against us? How do we handle attacks that are initiated by the devil and driven through the mouths and actions of human beings? Psalm 35, a psalm of David, gives us a really good plan of action.

"Plead my cause, O LORD, with them that strive with me: fight against them that fight against me. Take hold of shield and buckler, and stand up for mine help. Draw out also the spear, and stop the way against them that persecute me: say unto my soul, I am thy salvation." Psalm 35:1-3

The key to victory and being happy when faced with adversity or an adversary is knowing what the Bible says. If you are not a student of the Bible, you'll never amass enough spiritual knowledge and truth to be able to judge. This is a problem in the church today.

Caleb Bell of the Religious News Services wrote an article a while back about Christians and their Bibles. Here's what he said their survey revealed.

1. More than 57% of youth 18-28 read their Bibles only three times per year.
2. Only 26% of Americans said they read their Bibles every week…
3. 88% of respondents said they own a Bible.
4. There are 4.4 Bibles, on the average in every household of those that responded to the survey.

It is clear by the above statistics that most Christians are not equipped to do battle with the enemy of their soul. Plus, they have no idea about spiritual armor that is fashioned by God just for them.

The Armor of God is listed in Ephesians 6:10-18, Paul describes this resource that God makes available to his children.

Paul writes, *"For we do not wrestle against flesh and blood, but against principalities, against powers, against the rulers of the darkness of this age, against spiritual hosts of wickedness in the heavenly places. Therefore, take up the whole armor of God, that you may be able to withstand in the evil day, and having done all, to stand."*

One habit that every believer needs to develop is focusing on Ephesians 6:10–18 and "getting dressed" spiritually every day. It would go a long way to giving victory over the devil and his schemes. Here Paul states that, while we walk in the flesh (we are living and breathing in this human body), we do not war according to the flesh (we can't fight spiritual battles with fleshly weapons).

Instead, as we focus on the resources and weapons of spiritual strength, we can see God giving us victory. No demonic stronghold can withstand praying Christians wearing the full armor of God, battling with the Word of God, and empowered by his Spirit. Freedom From Demon Bondage Excerpts from CBN.org Website Article

Here are the pieces of God's armor that appear in Ephesians 6:14-17

1. Stand therefore, having your **loins girt about with truth**,
2. And having on the **breastplate of righteousness;**
3. And your **feet shod with the preparation of the gospel of peace**;
4. Above all, taking the **shield of faith,** wherewith ye shall be able to quench all the fiery darts of the wicked.
5. And take the **helmet of salvation**,
6. and the **sword of the Spirit**, which is the word of God
7. Note that we are to be strong *"in the Lord"* and *"in the power of His might."* We do not take on demonic strongholds in our own strength. We protect ourselves with the first five pieces of defensive armor and wield the one offensive weapon—the sword of the Spirit, which is the Word of God.

Note that we are to be strong *"in the Lord"* and *"in the power of His might."* We do not take on demonic strongholds in our own strength. We protect ourselves with the first five pieces of defensive armor and wield the one offensive weapon—the sword of the Spirit, which is the Word of God.

The Bible makes it clear that there are demons, or evil spirits, in the world, that interfere in people's lives (Ephesians 6:11-19). Evil forces, or powers, influence and control the minds of individuals, bring sickness and cause undesirable behavior, inability to function normally, and even suicide. As a result of these forces, people can become a danger to themselves as well as others.

However, the Holy Spirit guides us into all truth. He empowers us, and intercedes for us. He also gives us spiritual gifts, such as discerning of spirits, for our welfare and that of others (I Corinthians 12; Mark 16:9- 20).

Your greatest need is to continually study God's Word. Meditate upon the promises of God both day and night (Joshua 1:8) to put on the whole armor of God that you might be able to effectively overcome the forces of evil.

Jesus answered Satan with the Word of God (Luke 4:1-13*). You can do the same. Pray without ceasing (I Thessalonians 5:17) and get into a local church fellowship for further ministry (Hebrews 10:25).

VICTORS OR VICTIMS

Overcoming the enemy requires certain basic knowledge. As we have seen, 57% of all adult Christians read their Bibles only four or less times per year. It's hard to be a Victor with such little preparation. However, here are a few points that will aid in your search to move from a Victim to a Victor.

1. You must understand that the battle belongs to the Lord. He defeated Satan on the cross and rose from the dead victorious over death, hell and the grave. He died for our sins so we could be free from its bondage.
2. The enemy is real, just unseen with the physical eye. Yet, like the wind, that we cannot see, we both see and feel its effects. So it is with evil. We know it is there.
3. We must acknowledge that we are at war with evil forces. Denial doesn't keep us from getting hurt.
4. We must gather together the weapons of our warfare and learn how and when to use them.
5. We must develop a warier attitude and be willing to fight at a moment's notice.
6. We must know that our spiritual authority is Jesus, and become secure in his love.

7. We must learn the "Wiles" (Tricks) of the devil so we won't become a victim of them.

TWO PRIMARY ERRORS
Got/Questions.org

There are two primary errors when it comes to spiritual warfare—over-emphasis and under-emphasis. Some blame every sin, every conflict, and every problem on demons that need to be cast out. Others completely ignore the spiritual realm and the fact that the Bible tells us our battle is against spiritual powers.

The key to successful spiritual warfare is finding the biblical balance. Jesus sometimes cast demons out of people; other times he healed people with no mention of the demonic.

The apostle Paul instructs Christians to wage war against the sin in themselves (Romans 6) and warns us to oppose the schemes of the devil (Ephesians 6:10–18). Ephesians 6:10–12 says,

"Finally, be strong in the Lord and in his mighty power. Put on the full armor of God so that you can take your stand against the devil's schemes. For our struggle is not against flesh and blood, but against the rulers, against the authorities, against the powers of this dark world and against the spiritual forces of evil in the heavenly realms."

This text teaches some crucial truths: we can only stand strong in the Lord's power, it is God's armor that protects us and our battle is ultimately against spiritual forces of evil.

We are to pray in the power and will of the Holy Spirit. Jesus is our ultimate example of resisting temptation in spiritual warfare. Observe how Jesus handled direct attacks from Satan when he was tempted in the wilderness (Matthew 4:1–11). Each temptation was combated with the words "it is written."

The Word of the living God is the most powerful weapon against the temptations of the devil. *"I have hidden your word in my heart that I might not sin against you"* (Psalm 119:11).

I Peter 5:9 tells us that we are to resist the devil steadfastly in the faith. That means to use the Word of God against him in a constant array of spiritual mortars that are launched from our, "It Is Written" gun, just like Jesus did. If it becomes necessary, and it will, to speak to the demon force attacking you, do so "In the Name of Jesus". You do have the spiritual power to bind those forces and cast them out.

THE KEYS TO SUCCESS IN SPIRITUAL WARFARE

- We rely on God's power, not our own.
- We put on the whole armor of God.
- We draw on the power of Scripture—the Word of God is the Spirit's sword.
- We pray in perseverance and holiness, making our appeal to God.
- We stand firm (Ephesians 6:13–14);
- We submit to God;
- We resist the devil's work (James 4:7), *knowing that the Lord of hosts is our protector. "Truly He is my rock and my salvation; He is my fortress; I will never be shaken"* (Psalm 62:2).

There are many ways of dealing with adversity and those adversaries that come after us. You can put your head in the sand and not acknowledge it. You can reclassify it so it is not a threat. (Good luck with that) You can descend into denial and say that it doesn't exist. You can agree with your adversary and fall under his oppression and be tormented. Finally, you can fight the good fight of faith and resist your adversary at every turn. Listen again to what the apostle Peter said.

"Be sober, be vigilant; because your adversary the devil, as a roaring lion, walketh about, seeking whom he may devour: Whom resist steadfast in the faith, knowing that the same afflictions are accomplished in your brethren that are in the world." **I Peter 5:8**

Being truly happy is to know that you are an overcomer. Because you stand on the Word of God and resist the devil, you are free to live out the destiny God chose for you from the foundation of the world. This is true happiness.

CHAPTER SIX:
HAPPINESS THROUGH RESTING

There is a rest that God has provided for his children. However, this rest is only for those who walk with the Lord by faith. If you are a," sometimes" Christian with very little Biblical knowledge, you will most likely miss out on this type of rest.

One just doesn't stumble into the rest of God. The Lord has to lead you there. That means you have to be tuned into hearing his voice and willing to obey his commands. Otherwise, you will stray off in another direction. God must above all else, lead you. Now let's look at the scriptural support for such a notion.

"The Lord is my shepherd; I shall not want. He makes me to lie down in green pastures: he leadeth me beside the still waters. He restores my soul: he leadeth me in the paths of righteousness for his name's sake. Yea, though I walk through the valley of the shadow of death, I will fear no evil: for thou art with me; thy rod and thy staff they comfort me. Thou prepareth a table before me in the presence of my enemies: thou anointest my head with oil; my cup runneth over. Surely goodness and mercy shall follow me all the days of my life: and I will dwell in the house of the Lord forever." **Psalm 23**

Psalm 23 is probably the most well-known text in the Holy Scriptures. This is a most beloved psalm and has been quoted in almost every conceivable venue where people need hope. Many a soldier has carried it into battle or placed it next to his heart in a frightening foxhole. Hospitals and funeral homes are also often places of recital.

There was a time when every school child would learn it and say it as a daily routine. Sadly, those days are mostly gone because of our government's hatred of all things godly. However, disdain for the Bible does not diminish the spiritual impact made by its words.

Some folks fear turning their lives over to God because he might lead them somewhere they do not want to go. The 23rd psalm tells us that being led by God is a rewarding experience. We end up in green pastures (Prosperity) and lie down by still waters (Peace-no confusion); Our souls (Mind, Will & Emotions) are restored;

The fear of evil fades away; Goodness and mercy follow us through life; We even have a feast right in the midst of our enemies and finally we dwell with the lord forever. That's a pretty good deal, don't you think?

If we are looking to be happy, this is the way to go. We rest in the finished work of Jesus on the cross and trust that God will lead us away from harm. However, *God's Rest Is Not for Everyone.*

God does not lead the masses into his rest. He leads his Children. He must be your shepherd. That makes you, his sheep. Being a sheep has certain indicators that prove you are really a sheep and not a wolf:

1. Sheep hear their Shepherd's voice.
2. Sheep come to their Shepherd's call.
3. Sheep do not question their Shepherd's commands.
4. Sheep know when the wolf is near and cries for the Shepherd

The atheist, agnostic, pantheist, all others that reject Jesus Christ as well as disobedient Christians do not and will not follow his lead. Thus, they miss the rest of God.

JOHN MARINELLI

GOD'S PROMISE OF REST
Hebrews 4:1-11

"Therefore, since a promise remains of entering his rest, let us fear lest any of you seem to have come short of it. For indeed the gospel was preached to us as well as to them; but the word, which they heard did not profit them, not being mixed with faith in those who heard it. For we who have believed do enter that rest, as he has said: although the works were finished from the foundation of the world. "So I swore in My wrath, 'They shall not enter My rest, For He has spoken in a certain place of the seventh day in this way: "And God rested on the seventh day from all his works"; and again, in this place: "They shall not enter My rest."

Since therefore it remains that some must enter it, and those to whom it was first preached did not enter because of disobedience, again He designates a certain day, saying in David, "Today," after such a long time, as it has been said:

"Today, if you will hear his voice, do not harden your hearts."

For if Joshua had given them rest, then he would not afterward have spoken of another day. There remains therefore a rest for the people of God. For he who has entered His rest has himself also ceased from his works as God did from His.

Let us therefore be diligent to enter that rest, lest anyone fall according to the same example of disobedience."

We are encouraged to rest from all our works because God rested from all his works. The promise from God is that we can really enter into his rest and because he did, we can too from all of our works.

However, sometimes we have to labor to enter in. Why? Because sometimes we get so caught up in what we are doing that it's really hard to just sit back and leave it up to God.

Someone may be wondering what is, "all our works." It is not getting up and going to work every day or being a reliable husband or wife.

The rest is from trying to attain salvation by our own efforts. God took care of that in his master plan before the foundation of the world. His redemptive plan for man was to sacrifice his only Son as a penalty for sin and offer his salvation to all who would believe. **(John 3:16)**

To rest then is to believe that Jesus was sacrificed for our sin and accept him as our savior. We are to put our trust in him and stop trying to buy God's favor with good works. **(Ephesians 2:8-9)**

That which we let go of is the anxiety, fear, confusion, worry and control over our own lives. We are to step off the throne of our life. That seat is now reserved for Jesus. We can trust him because he said from the cross; **"It Is Finished"** which fulfilled God's rest from all his works on the 7th day of creation.

He already made plans for us to rest in him. Those that see this truth also rest from all their works which are being anxious, fearful, stressed, depressed and all the negative worries of life. They realize that God is in control and they do not have to labor any more. This is the basis for Romans 8:28-30 where Paul, the apostle, tells the church that God works all things together for good for those who are called according to his purposes and reverence (Fear) him. The inference is that they do not have to worry or fret about anything.

Hebrews 4 is the definitive passage regarding Jesus as our Sabbath rest. The writer to the Hebrews exhorts his readers to "enter in" to the Sabbath rest provided by Christ. After three chapters of telling them that Jesus is superior to the angels and that he is our Apostle and High Priest, he pleads with them to not harden their hearts against him, as their fathers hardened their hearts against the Lord in the wilderness. Because of their unbelief, God denied that generation access to the holy land, saying, *"They shall not enter into My rest"* **Hebrews 3:11.**

In the same way, the writer to the Hebrews begs his readers not to make the same mistake by rejecting God's Sabbath rest in Jesus Christ. "There remains, then, a Sabbath-rest for the people of God; for anyone who enters God's rest also rests from his own work, just as God did from his. Let us, therefore, make every effort to enter that rest, so that no one will fall by following their example of disobedience" **Hebrews 4:9–11**

SPIRITUALLY SPEAKING

Now that I have shown the scripture in contest and explained the meaning of the text in Hebrews, let's look at the spiritual applications. As Christians, we have made Jesus Lord and seek to walk with him through this world. However, evil is on every side and it is hard to live out our faith in Christ. We strive to make ends meet. We worry over our children and their future. We hope that sickness or sorrow will not knock on our door. We are anxious, fearful, and when someone says to us, "How are you doing today", we reply with, "I am just hanging in there".

This is a word picture of a Christian without faith. They are doing just what the Old Testament saints did, not believing. Their unbelief kept them from entering into God's rest. We can fall into the same scenario and miss out on the promise. If we miss out, we remain in a state of turmoil and stay unhappy. If we believe and rest in the finished work of Jesus, we allow him to be Lord over our every situation. This is true happiness and that is our goal. Entering into God's rest takes away the pain and brings laughter.

HOW DO WE ENTER IN?

Our labor to enter in is believing. What do we believe? We believe that God rested on the 7th day from all his work. That means his master plan was complete. It means that God saw every need, every situation and every prayer in his foreknowledge and scheduled them for action.

The Law was seen long before it appeared. In the fullness of time, it came to expose sin and bring death to all that sin. **(Lev.18:20)** Accordingly, in the fullness of time, Christ came with a new law...the law of the Spirit of Life that brought us liberty and salvation. **(Romans 8:2)**

This new law set us free from the old one. However, both were in God's master plan waiting to be released. Thus, it is with our daily lives. We are in God's master plan and he works everything together for our good and his glory. **(Romans 8:28)** All we have to do is trust in Jesus; believe that he is in control; and wait for the manifestation of our deliverance/supply.

We enter in by faith and we remain at rest knowing that the battle is the Lord's and he is our shield against evil and lack in this life. He will provide. He will lead us to green pastures and still waters. He will restore our souls, just like the 23rd psalm says.

UNBELIEVING CHILDREN OF GOD

The Bible tells us that some of the Old Testament saints did not believe and they perished in the wilderness. They never entered the rest of God that was promised to them. They never entered the Promised Land. However, the amazing thing was that God still took care of them in the wilderness. Their shoes did not wear out. Nor did their clothing. They ate manna from heaven. No one was feeble in mind or spirit. They still died in the wilderness. Here's what this says to me:

1. Life can be good but you can still miss out on God's very best.
2. It is better to fear (reverence) God than to fear giants and men of power and authority that dwell in your future.
3. God's blessings are always connected with Faith. No faith, no promise, no divine destiny.
4. Fear will hinder faith. They are two sides to the same coin. But faith crushes fear and brings victory.

5. One's destiny rest in their own hands. We choose the path to walk in life and what lies at the end of the road. Life or death is in the power of our own choices.

6. God is looking for a partner to rule the earth and has chosen us, his children…those who are willing to stand with him.

Let us be clear as to the rest of God. It is all about our access to God and our personal salvation. We are resting from the quest to be good enough in the sight of God. We are resting from the idea that salvation is based upon our works, not God's grace. It's that simple, yet it is also that hard. It is hard to believe that God has accepted us even though we are of a sinful nature. Aren't we suppose to do good works, be as good as we can and pray a lot? That's all well and good but these things cannot get you a ticket to heaven. Believing in and adhering to what God has said will get you there.

LIVING IN GOD'S REST
A Word from Joyce Meyer

"When I'm *trying* to believe, I haven't entered God's rest. But when I *do* believe, I have complete rest in him. Living by faith is not a struggle—it's a rest. And you can enter into God's rest in every area of your life. I've discovered that the stress in my life is caused by the way I approach my circumstances and the attitude I have toward them. It was a turning point for me when I realized that the world will probably never change, but I could learn how to change the way I go about handling situations that are challenging.

One key to this is knowing that as believers in Christ, we are partners with God—we have a part and he has a part in everything he calls us to do. When we don't do the part, we can do and we try to do his part, that's when we live stressed-out with worry, fear, anxiety, frustration, no peace and no joy.

The reason this happens sometimes is because we think God needs our help. We meditate on the problem—rolling it over and over in our mind, worrying, and trying to figure out how things should work out. It's like we're telling God, "I kind of think you need my help, and I'm not sure you can take care of this situation, Lord."

We need to realize that worrying is useless! It's like sitting in a rocking chair, rocking all day, wearing yourself out and getting nowhere. Trusting God means we give up worrying, reasoning, and anxiety and we enter into his rest with simple childlike faith—we live by grace through faith!" (Excerpts from her article, "Living In God's Rest)

GOD MEANS WHAT HE SAYS

The greatest kind of relationship with God is the one where he takes care of you in this life and the one to come. That's what God is promising. This is what the scripture calls rest. But many of God's children, because they, for some reason or another won't believe that God means what he says.

It's really amazing that God offers all of this to his children and some just won't believe it. These folks find it easier to resist the goodness of God. One day they will face their heavenly Father and give an account for their unbelief. For now, they continue wandering in the wilderness of anxiety, confusion, depression and worry over every life situation, having no rest…no peace…and so the warning from the Spirit of God is **"Harden Not Your Hearts."** Don't be like unbelieving Israel and miss God's perfect rest.

BENEFITS OF ENTERING INTO GOD'S REST

When we enter into the rest of God, we benefit in these important ways:

1. **We have continual access into God's rest where we find peace and happiness.**

It's God's rest. That means he is at rest, knowing that his master plan is activated and being accomplished. If we know this, we can also rest, knowing that he is in control. The key is, who is in control of things, God or you? I say, keep the, "Continual Access" alive because we, being of a fallen nature, sometimes freak out and exit God's rest. However, having access all the time is the privilege of returning back to his rest anytime we want. *(Let us therefore come boldly unto the throne of grace, that we may obtain mercy, and find grace to help in time of need.")* **Hebrews 4:16** This is the foundation of our happiness and it flows out of our relationship with our Heavenly Father.

2. **We gain a new perspective on life and eternity.**

It's our life and we can live it anyway we so desire. Over the years, we form a perspective that drives our thought process and shapes our destiny. If that perspective is negative, we see life that way. We worry, get anxious, become fearful and generally live a defeated life. Becoming a Christian is just a title. It does not change you. You change you. How we see things is the motivator for how we act and speak and think. When we see that God is really in control, we start shifting our perspective from a negative to a positive. We begin to trust in Jesus and start saying that everything will work out. This changes our life dramatically. *"And we know that God causes all things to work together for good to those who love God, to those who are called according to His purpose."* **Romans 8:28** Here-in is happiness.

3. **We do not beat ourselves up when we fall short.**

When we realize that God is not kidding and life is not a video game. We discover his magnificent grace. He has forgiven us our trespasses. We are free to worship him and have fellowship through his Spirit. (***"If we confess our sins, he is faithful and just to forgive us our sins, and to cleanse us from all unrighteousness."***) **I John 1:9** Another great scriptural proof is **II Corinthians 5:21,** ***"For he hath made him to be sin for us, who knew no sin; that we might be made the righteousness of God in him."*** We can go on in life believing God that he is in control, even over our salvation.

4. **We start being who we are in Christ and not what others think we are.**

If you are truly saved by the blood of Jesus, you will become a "New Creature" so the Bible says, ***"Therefore if any man be in Christ, he is a new creature: old things are passed away; behold, all things are become new."*** **II Corinthian 5:17** What that new creature looks like is mostly a spiritual image and reflection of God. This can be seen by reading **Galatians 5:22**, which is: Love, Peace, Joy, Longsuffering, Self-Control, and all the other fruit of God's Spirit. The opinions of others, the critical attacks of Satan and all the rest just fall away. We do not dwell in them anymore. Our new man serves the lord with great Joy. This is true happiness.

5. **We have true fellowship with God and we rest in His grace.**

Does God talk to you? I hear his voice all the time. Wouldn't it be strange for a father to not talk to his children? What kind of father neglects his kids like that? God sees to it that we hear his voice and he always listens for ours. Remember, his Holy Spirit dwells within us and leads us along life's way. As we read the Bible, we learn of him. As we apply the truths found in the Bible, we grow in Faith and have fellowship with him. ***"The Spirit itself beareth witness with our spirit, that we are the children of God:"*** **Romans 8:16**

6. **We see God at work, fighting our battles for us. The battle is the Lords.**

If we are truly at rest, we do not fight every battle that comes our way. In fact, Paul tells us that we can simply resist the devil steadfast in the faith. ***"Be sober, be vigilant; because your adversary the devil, as a roaring lion, walketh about, seeking whom he may devour: Whom resist steadfast in the faith, knowing that the same afflictions are accomplished in your brethren that are in the world."*** **I Peter 5:8-9** We need to allow God to be God in our lives and keep him in control of things.

7. **We become more thankfully towards God as he reveals his will and shows us the way.**

As we rest in God, we grow in grace. We see his hand in our life and hear his voice. All of this makes us more thankful than ever before. Our thoughts move to an old expression that is found in **Psalm 124**,

"If it had not been the LORD who was on our side, now may Israel say; If it had not been the LORD who was on our side, when men rose up against us: Then they had swallowed us up quick, when their wrath was kindled against us: Then the waters had overwhelmed us, the stream had gone over our soul: Then the proud waters had gone over our soul. Blessed be the LORD, who hath not given us as a prey to their teeth. Our soul is escaped as a bird out of the snare of the fowlers: the snare is broken, and we are escaped. Our help is in the name of the LORD, who made heaven and earth."

Our praise and adoration for God is because we know that *"If it had not been the Lord"*, we would not have been able to stand.

I am sure you can find more benefits. Mine are just some that I know to be true.

There remains a rest for the children of God. It was born out of God's rest on the 7th day of creation when he rested from all his work. It is a

Sabbath Rest that was fulfilled in the person of Jesus Christ. This is the cradle for your happiness.

It was Jesus that completed the Law and opened up the door of grace for those who believed in him. He was the one that lived the life that God expected man to live, a righteous life.

He was the only one that could die for the sins of mankind, because he was, as it were, the spotless Lamb of God, that was foreshadowed in the Hebrew sacrifices of the Old Testament. It was he that became the Captain of our Salvation and Lord of Heaven and Earth.

To enter into God's rest is to receive Christ as Savior and Lord and to rest in his finished work of Grace. This entire concept of Rest is wrapped up in John's record of what Jesus said*...." For God so loved the world that He gave His only begotten Son, that whoever believes in Him should not perish but have everlasting life." * **John 3:16**

We know that we are in God's rest when we are not worrying; have no anxiety; have no fear of the future; when we are not striving to do good deeds to be accepted; when we are at peace, full of joy and love; have patience, and can see ourselves in eternity with Jesus. This is true happiness.

The only thing we are instructed to fear is unbelief. We always want to believe regardless of what we see or feel. God is always with us and he alone is in control.

This is the perspective that should rule our lives and shape our actions. Unbelief has no place in our Spiritual walk with Jesus. We walk by faith and not by sight. **II Corinthians 5:7**

CHAPTER SEVEN:
THERE IS A REASON FOR EVERYTHING

There is no way to really be happy if we do not realize that everything has a reason. There is a reason for that. *A Reason for What?* A reason for everything that comes into our lives. We may not know what that reason is but there is still a reason for its existence.

Have you ever wondered why things happen? Things like someone pulling out onto the highway right in front of you and then slowing down… or like you can't get your car started and are late for work…or having a meeting downtown and not having to go. We are going to look at some different scenarios and possible outcomes. We will be speculating on some and showing facts on others. Here's a real live example from the Bible. It's found in **John 9:1-23…**

"Now as *Jesus* passed by, He saw a man who was blind from birth. And his disciples asked him, saying, "Rabbi, who sinned, this man or his parents, that he was born blind?" Jesus answered, "Neither this man nor his parents sinned, but that the works of God should be revealed in him. I must work the works of him who sent me while it is day; *the* night is coming when no one can work. As long as I am in the world, I am the light of the world."

When he had said these things, he spat on the ground and made clay with the saliva; and he anointed the eyes of the blind man with the clay. And he said to him, "Go, wash in the pool of Siloam" (which is translated, Sent). So he went and washed, and came back seeing.

Therefore, the neighbors and those who previously had seen that he was blind said, "Is not this he who sat and begged?" Some said, "This is he." Others *said,* "he is like him." He said, "I am *he.*" Therefore, they said to him, "How were your eyes opened?" He answered and said, "A man called Jesus made clay and anointed my eyes and said to me, "Go to the pool of Siloam and wash." So I went and washed, and I received sight." Then they said to him, "Where is he?" He said, "I do not know." They brought him who formerly was blind to the Pharisees. Now it was a Sabbath when Jesus made the clay and opened his eyes. Then the Pharisees also asked him again how he had received his sight. He said to them, "He put clay on my eyes, and I washed, and I see."

Therefore, some of the Pharisees said, "This man is not from God, because he does not keep the Sabbath." Others said, "How can a man who is a sinner do such signs?" And there was a division among them.

They said to the blind man again, "What do you say about him because he opened your eyes?" He said, "he is a prophet." But the Jews did not believe concerning him, that he had been blind and received his sight, until they called the parents of him who had received his sight. And they asked them, saying, "Is this your son, who you say was born blind? How then does he now see?"

His parents answered them and said, "We know that this is our son, and that he was born blind; but by what means he now sees we do not know, or who opened his eyes we do not know. He is of age; ask him. He will speak for himself." His parents said these *things* because they feared the Jews, for the Jews had agreed already that if anyone confessed *that he was* Christ, he would be put out of the synagogue. Therefore, his parents said, "He is of age; ask him."

Did you get the picture? Jesus was walking by with his disciples and saw a blind man. His disciples wanted to know why this guy was blind from his birth. Jesus said it was because the works of God should be revealed in him. He was also careful to explain that it was not the guy's fault or his parents.

So he, the blind man, went through life begging for alms and living in a world of darkness until one ordinary day of doing the same old things, God showed up and demonstrated his power. Jesus healed him and he could see.

There Was A Reason For His Blindness. There is always a reason for what happens to us. The sovereignty of God was at play as God intervened in someone's life. You can bet your bottom dollar that when God steps in, he has a good reason for doing so.

It is very comforting to me to know that I am not subject to a life that is no more than a random flow of chaos. There is always a reason for what happens and I can thank God that he is on top of things, intervening as needed to bring about blessings instead of sorrow.

It's important to see what happened as a result of Jesus' Miracle.

1. The blind man now sees clearly.
2. All his friends see or hear about the miracle and are amazed.
3. His parents are glad.
4. The religious leaders are angry with Jesus and excommunicate the blind man from the temple.
5. The blind man is now an evangelist of sorts as he tells how he can see.
6. The man's lifestyle has changed dramatically and that change has touched the lives of others is a significant way.

Now we can see why, *There Is A Reason For That*.

Unexpected Delays Can Have a Good Outcome

My wife's brother lives in the New York area. On 9/11 he was scheduled for an early morning meeting down town at the Twin Towers. His meeting was canceled at the last minute and he didn't go. The day of the meeting, terrorist flew hijacked passenger Jets into the Twin Towers and the Pentagon and more than 3600 people died.

Is the canceled meeting just a coincidence or an intervention of God? He very well could have been killed had the meeting taken place. He lives today, very possibly because his meeting was canceled. *There was a reason for that.*

Evaluating The Possibilities

It is important to realize that most folks see only what they want to see. Two people can review the same evidence and come to very different conclusions. It's all in your belief system and how you see things. In the Biblical example above, some said the man was the same one that they saw begging before but others wouldn't go that far and said he looked similar.

The religious leaders were stuck in their own dogma and fought to be politically correct. We, as Christians, believe that God is always with us and if we have read the scriptures, we surely have come across **Psalm 34:7**, *"The angel of the LORD encampeth round about them that fear him, and delivereth them."*

We believe that it is indeed possible for God to intervene into our daily routine to protect and even deliver us from evil. We are always evaluating the possibilities and looking for the hand of God.

I know what you will most likely say, "What about when tragedy strikes and the outcome is not what we desire? I have had several folks tell me of freak accidents where their loved ones have died or become crippled. How does that work within the sovereignty of God?

These things are hard to deal with because they happen to us. Nevertheless, *"There Is A Reason For That"*. The truth is… God does not generate every happening. We generate some from our own free will. Others do too.

Therefore, the reasons for an occurrence can differ depending on the source. Ask the drunk that runs over a little kid. Ask the terrorist that blows up a plane. Ask the construction guy that builds a shabby building that falls down in the 1st severe storm.

God does not generate them and it was not his will that they happen. He allows us to be a free moral agent and gives us a free will to do whatever we want. However, he also holds us accountable for our actions. God has promised us that he will work everything together for good. Hear what **Romans 8:28** says, *"And we know that all things work together for good to them that love God, to them who are the called according to his purpose."*

So, some things are born out of God's divine will. Others come from us. Yet other things happen as a result of nature and weather patterns. Finally, there are those things that come from our adversary, the devil. Hear what Peter said:

"Be sober, be vigilant; because your adversary the devil, as a roaring lion, walketh about, seeking whom he may devour: Whom resist stedfast in the faith, knowing that the same afflictions are accomplished in your brethren that are in the world." **I Peter 5:8-9**

The Underlying Premise

The underlying premise to, **"There's A Reason For That"** is as follows:

1. The belief that God is good.
2. The understanding that God wants us to be happy.
3. The words of Jesus in **John 10:10b**, "I have come that they (Us) might have life and that they (us) may have *it* more abundantly"
4. That Jesus will never leave us.
5. That God's angel sets up his camp of warring angels all around us because we reverence God.
6. That God is really for his children and not against them.

7. That we can evaluate the reasons, looking for the hand of God.

Judging Before the Results Are In

Some folks make a judgment before the results are fully known. One year, we lost two dogs and a cat to sickness and disease. It all happened within a 30-45 day period. Our hearts were broken and, as is natural, we questioned why?

It was easy to blame God because he is in control of everything, right? He could have intervened and saved our precious pets. However, he did not… or did he?

Our emotions raged and we kept hearing the thoughts of Satan that said how bad God was to allow this to happen. Fortunately, we stayed in faith, believing that God is good and he was not in the business of killing our pets.

To believe what was racing through our emotions would be to believe a lie because we know who God is and such an act would be out of character for him. Plus, we read in the John 10:10 that, *"The thief does not come except to steal, and to kill, and to destroy."* We quickly realized that this thing was not from our Heavenly Father.

We still struggled with Why? But withheld our judgment saying, *"There Must Be A Reason For That"*. We just don't know it as yet.

Later, we learned that the dog food, even though it was a better mix and more costly, had several recalls due to bacteria problems and that the vet we were using at the time had no real answers.

Our final conclusion was to say, we don't really know except, the animals were suffering and God took them before they got worse. He spared us the continual agony of watching them slowly die and spared our beloved pets the ever-worsening pain.

So finally, we could put it to rest that God was not at fault and our animals are now in his loving care.

I know it is hard not to blame God but it is important to look to him for answers, realizing that he is on our side and will be forever.

A "Reason" Implies A Plan

If there is a reason for everything that happens, is there also a plan? The Bible teaches that God has "Foreknowledge" of everything, every event. It also teaches that God is "Sovereign." That means that God's master plan was designed after every happening in every century, with every person, animal, weather, etc. was identified by its corresponding reason.

Foreknowledge... is the ability to know what will take place and the results of those events before they take place. God is all-knowing and all powerful. He is the only one that can judge the intent of the heart. God saw it all before the foundation of the world and designed his Master Plan accordingly.

Sovereignty... is God's absolute right to rule over his creation. *"So shall my word be that goeth forth out of my mouth: it shall not return unto me void, but it shall accomplish that which I please, and it shall prosper in the thing whereto I sent it."* **Isaiah 55:11**

God's work, from which he rested on the 7th day, was not just the creation of the planets, the universes, and the great expanse. It was also to make every decision as to his own will without violating man's free will choices.

God, in that decision making process, took into account many different things, including:

1. **Fulfilling Romans 8:28** which says, *"And we know that all things work together for good to those who love God, to those who are the called according to His purpose."*

2. Setting appointments for folks to die. *"And as it is appointed for men to die once, but after this the judgment"* **Hebrews 9:27**

3. Sending Jesus to earth. *"But when the fullness of the time was come, God sent forth his Son, made of a woman, made under the law, to redeem them that were under the law, that we might receive the adoption of sons and because ye are sons, God hath sent forth the Spirit of his Son into your hearts, crying, Abba, Father. Wherefore thou art no more a servant, but a son; and if a son, then an heir of God through Christ.* **Galatians 4:6-7**

These are but a few of the millions of decisions relative to God's Sovereignty. However, this is the only way God could truly give man a free will and to allow him to be a free moral agent. In doing so, all of life has a cause and effect which says. *"There is a reason for everything?* There is a master plan that retains God's Sovereignty and man's free will.

Some More Biblical Examples

Jesus, An Excellent Example... I'd like to use Jesus as an example of, "There's A Reason For That". You 're aware that he was and still is the Only Begotten Son of God, sent by him as a penalty for sin and Savor for all who believe in him? **John 3:16** You should also be aware that the Romans crucified him and put him in a borrowed grave.

Picture yourself there, seeing his miracles, hearing his, "Gospel of the Kingdom" and actually seeing him being crucified on the cross of Calvary. What would you think? He is now dead and all that he said apparently died with him. That's what some of the disciples thought. At the garden, when they came for Jesus, they all ran away in fear. Only John was there at the cross. Peter denied knowing Jesus three times before Jesus went to the cross.

If I would have told the disciples, "There is a reason for that", they would have thought I was crazy. But there was a reason for the crucifixion.

They didn't know it then but after Jesus rose from the dead and showed them his hands and side, they knew. It all became clear. It was God's master plan being worked out so he could redeem his children and save them from his own sentence of death. With the eyes of man, this would seem like a tragedy.

However, the true reason was not apparent. It was actually hidden from the world but known by the believers. The world rejoiced at the death of Christ but God had the last laugh. He used their evil deeds to bring about something good, our redemption and planned it all before the foundation of the world.

Joseph, Another Biblical Example... You know the story, how Joseph's brothers sold him into slavery and told his father that he was dead. That he ended up in Egypt and because the Pharaoh's right-hand man. That, because of a famine, his brothers came to Egypt looking to buy food and came face to face with Joseph. This is what

Joseph says to his brothers. *"But as for you, ye thought evil against me; but God meant it unto good, to bring to pass, as it is this day, to save much people alive."* **Genesis 50:20**

All of this was in God's master plan just waiting to be enacted. It's also a clear example that the story is not over until it is over. There was a reason that Joseph was sold into slavery by his brothers. It wasn't what God wanted but was the very thing God used to save Jacob's family and continue his will.

A "What If" Scenario

I have pointed out Biblical examples and even a real-life story to illustrate, "There's A Reason For That". Now let's take a look at a hypothetical. I will give you the scenario and multiple choices. See if you can pick the right answer.

You are driving too fast to work. You are late and you are trying to make up time so you won't be that late. You are on a two-lane highway with a fair amount of traffic.

A farmer pulls out in front of you. He is hauling a trailer full of watermelon. He is going slower than the speed limit, forcing you to slow down. There is too much traffic coming the other way for you to pass. All you can do is poke along behind the farmer.

"There's A Reason For That"...What reason could there be for this happening to you?

a.) Maybe there's a cop hiding down the road and if you were speeding you probably would have been caught.

b.) Maybe an accident was about to happen that would have involved you had you kept on at a faster pace but because you slowed down, there was no accident.

c.) Maybe you have a problem getting angry too quickly at things and God uses things like this so you will learn patience.

d.) Maybe all the above is applicable.

e.) Maybe none of the above applies.

The, "What If scenario" answer is **"e"** but does it really matter why a thing happens? We know that God has put his Holy Spirit into our hearts as a seal of our redemption and he will do what is best for us. *"Now he which established us with you in Christ, and hath anointed us, is God; who hath also sealed us, and given the earnest of the Spirit in our hearts."* **II Corinthians 1:21-22**

The point is... there is a reason for things happening. They just don't happen on their own. Sometimes they are sent by God to teach us, protect us and keep us walking in his grace.

There are a million reasons why things happen in life. Trying to figure them all out can be exhausting. Knowing the possible sources can be comforting but still frustrating. All I need to know is my Heavenly Father is in control of my life and what happens to me. He has my best interest at heart.

I have his Spirit to lead me out of harm's way and into his blessings. If I should encounter things that go against my will and frustrate me, I can use them to cultivate patience and my spiritual walk. I can also reject them as being an attack from the devil.

The source or reason for them entering my reality is not important. What is important is that the things I experience do not break my stride as I walk with the Lord.

I know that Jesus came that I might have life and that life would be more abundant that ever before. **John 10:10b**

I also know that I am aware of the tricks of the devil and can resist him and the things he brings my way by standing in faith against him.

God is good. He is the Father of all life and is the very essence of Love. We should trust him in all things and rely on him to get us through the good times and even the bad times. He will, if we reverence him, work everything together for our good. So, keep looking up and drop pre-judging of every little thing. Relax and enjoy life.

It is God's will that you be happy.

CHAPTER EIGHT:
STAYING HAPPY 24/7

We all want to stay happy 24/7, right? That seems almost impossible. Why can't I stay happy all the time? I think I can answer that for you. It's because you are a human being, not a robot.

We humans are a funny bunch. We labor over every passing emotion. Sometimes we are ok, feeling good about ourselves and sometimes we are just not with it. Happiness is just not stable enough to keep us going all the time. Even when we get enough sleep and have a positive outlook on life, we often fall prey to doubt, guilt, inadequacy and other harmful emotions.

We need a life coach that is a cheerleader who can constantly be there to hold us up. Oh, that's right. We have one, the Holy Spirit. Jesus said, *"But the Comforter, which is the Holy Ghost, whom the Father will send in my name, he shall teach you all things, and bring all things to your remembrance, whatsoever I have said unto you."* John 14:26

This book is a study of what the Bible says about being happy. I do not want to deviate too much from the scriptures and my personal experiences. However, sometimes the secular (non-Christian) references can shed practical light on any given subject. Therefore, I have added a few comments and observations to my text so you get the full body of knowledge. Here we go...

Martin Seligman, the founding father of positive psychology, tells us that true happiness is not unchangeable but something even flexible. It is something that we can work on and ultimately strive towards. Although this is not a Biblical reference, the man is still right. It is obvious, at least to me, that my happiness shifts from day to day and even moment by moment depending on what is going on in my thought life.

I guess it is ok to say that we cannot always apply the techniques that we know will help. We have or know the tools but sometimes we just can't seem to use them. Our minds wander and we drift off into a world of negativity or fear or even demonic traps and snares. I guess the Old Testament prophet, Isiah, was right when he said, "All we like sheep *have gone astray; we have turned everyone to his own way;" (The good news is that God placed our iniquity/sin on Jesus at the cross) and the Lord hath laid on him the iniquity of us all."* Isaiah 53:6

Studies have demonstrated that the way we respond to the circumstances of our lives has more influence on our happiness than the events themselves. Experiencing stress, sadness and anxiety in the short term doesn't mean we can't be happy in the long term. This is because we are ever striving to achieve and the goal of being happy is attainable, so says the Bible.

Martin Seligman presents two viewpoints. He says**, " p**hilosophically speaking there are two paths to feeling happy, the hedonistic and the eudaimonic."

Hedonists take the view that in order to live a happy life we must maximize pleasure and avoid pain. This view is about satisfying human appetites and desires, but it is often short lived.

In contrast, the eudaimonic approach takes the long view. It argues that we should live authentically and for the greater good. We should pursue meaning and potential through kindness, justice, honesty and courage.

If we see happiness in the hedonistic sense, then we have to continue to seek out new pleasures and experiences in order to "prop up" our happiness. We will also try to minimize unpleasant and painful feelings in order to keep our mood high.

If we take the eudaimonic approach, however, we strive for meaning, using our strengths to contribute to something greater than ourselves. This may involve unpleasant experiences and emotions at times, but often leads to deeper levels of joy and contentment. So, leading a happy life is not about avoiding hard times; it is about being able to respond to adversity in a way that allows you to grow from the experience. (Excerpts from the January 2018 Online Science of Happiness article titled True Happiness Isn't About Being Happy All of the Time)

This eudaimonic approach is closely aligned with the Bible in that it supports a healthy long-term effort to apply Bible truths to any given situation.

Both definitions are understood to be correct and speak of different realities. But are they really that different? I don't think so.

After all, a long-term experience of life satisfaction is almost certainly made up of many short-term feelings of joy and pleasure. Does that mean every day is a great day with no trials, temptations, or downturns? Certainly not. But it does mean when we look back at the many seasons of life, we can look back satisfied at how we navigated them.

The long-term feeling of life satisfaction is most experienced when we embrace the emotion of joy in the here and now. And we accomplish that by taking steps each day to be happy.

Here are some tips on how to be happier starting today by Joshua Becker, Christian Pastor & Minimalist.

(Note: Minimalism is not a religion, cult or weird thing. It is simply a lifestyle where those who embrace it strive to live as simply say they can. They say that they ffree themselves from the accumulation of stuff so they can be free to do more activities, following God would be one.)

1. Choose happiness

The most important thing to realize about happiness is that it is not an outcome of current circumstances. Just the opposite, **happiness is a choice**. Is this easier on some days than others? Absolutely. But if you get caught in the trap of thinking your circumstances need to change before you can be happy, you'll never, ever get there.

2. Focus on the good

There are good things in your life right now: you are alive, you are fed, you are healthy, you have family and friends, and you have opportunities each day to pursue meaningful work. Maybe not all of those are true for you right now, but certainly some of them are—which means there is good in your life that you can focus on.

Marine Sgt. Jonny Joseph Jones lost both of his legs in an explosion while serving in Afghanistan. I was struck by a quote of his I saw recently. He said this, "People ask how I stay so positive after losing my legs… I simply ask how they stay so negative when they have both of theirs."

Happiness is about perspective and if you're looking for reasons to be happy, you'll probably find them. Happy people focus on positive thoughts.

3. Stop comparing

No matter how you choose to define happiness—short-term or long-term—comparison will rob you of it. Whether we compare our finances, our body type, our vacations, our talents, our house size or our shoe size, there are no winners in the game of comparison. But here's the good news: Nobody is forcing you to play! You can stop any time you want. Be grateful for what you have, appreciate who you are, work hard every day to live your best life, and **stop comparing yourself to others**.

4. Practice gratitude and generosity

In the world of positive psychology, there are a few themes that emerge every time happiness is studied. Among those recurring themes, we find gratitude and generosity.

Both of which can only be understood correctly when we see them as disciplines rather than responses. A discipline is something we practice regardless of our circumstances. If you are waiting for enough money to become generous, you'll never get there. Likewise, if you are waiting for everything to be perfect to be grateful, you'll never experience it. Choose to be thankful today. And choose to be generous with your time and money. Making them both a discipline in your life will result in a happier today… and tomorrow.

5. Don't pursue physical possessions

Possessions are necessary for life, but our society has seemed to confuse consumerism with happiness. Marketers work hard to convince us their products are not just needed for life, but that they are essential for happiness.

Slowly but surely, we begin to believe their empty promises and waste our lives pursuing things that can never satisfy. We sacrifice time, money, energy, and focus chasing and accumulating things we do not need.

These excess possessions add stress, worry, and burden onto our lives. Want to become a bit happier today? Go declutter a closet or drawer and start to challenge consumerism in your life.

6. Be present in your relationships

Robert J. Waldinger is an American psychiatrist and Professor at Harvard Medical School where he is best known for directing the world's longest-running longitudinal study tracking the health and mental well-being of a group of 724 American men for 76 years. One thing that he has learned, and has been confirmed by studies elsewhere, is that relationships hold the key to happiness:

Close relationships, more than money or fame, are what keep people happy throughout their lives, the study revealed. Those ties protect people from life's discontents, help to delay mental and physical decline, and are better predictors of long and happy lives than social class, IQ, or even genes. We don't get to control every aspect of our relationships (we didn't choose our family, for example). But we can all take steps to be a good friend. And good friends tend to attract healthy community.

7. Develop healthy habits

Annie Dillard is credited for saying, "How we spend our days is, of course, how we spend our lives." And she is right. Our lives are filled with days, our days are filled with hours, and this present hour is filled with whatever you chose so why not fill it with healthy habits that add value to your life. Spend time outside. Eat healthy. Exercise regularly. Quit smoking. Put down your cell phone. Obsess less. Work hard. Pray often. And get enough sleep.

8. Look outside yourself

The pursuit of self comes natural to us. We don't need to be reminded to pursue our own self-interests. We pursue self-survival, self-promotion, self-actualization and self-exaltation as if it is hardwired in our genes.

But the **most** efficient pathway to lasting happiness and fulfillment is not to look only at your own interests, but also to the interests of others. When we shift our focus off of ourselves, we live lives of greater meaning and greater contribution. When we serve others without concern over what we might receive in return, we experience the beauty of selfless love. The size of our universe (and happiness) begins to expand exponentially. *(Look not every man on his own things, but* every *man also on the things of others*. Philippians 2:4)

All of the above are examples of good common sense. There is no mystery. However, some folks miss it altogether. It is no small thing that happiness is pursued by so many. Let's make sure we find it—in both the short term and the long term.

WHAT MAKES US HAPPY
(Excerpts from Johnathan Kingsford's March 2021 Health Hackers Lab article)

Behavioral scientists have spent a lot of time studying what makes us happy and what doesn't make us happy. We know happiness can predict health and longevity, and happiness scales can be used to measure social progress and the success of public policies. But happiness isn't something that just happens to you. Everyone has the power to make small changes in our behavior, our surroundings and our relationships that can help set us on course for a happier life. (*Tara Parker-Pope NY Times article on how to be happy*)

Small changes are actually baby steps. Most folks can't change everything at once. It's just too expensive. But you can take baby steps. Here are a few to consider:

1. Throw away papers that clutter up your desk. Make your environment neat and tidy. It will make you feel better and that trends to being happy.
2. Have a yard or garage sale and get rid of stuff. This will open up space and will be pleasing to the eye.
3. Re-decorate your house or bedroom. It will change how you feel about being in that space.
4. Go a different way to work or church just to change your routine. You will feel like you are on an adventure.
5. Change your mindset. We are by nature negative, so don't be. Start thinking of good things to do. The Bible says, *"Finally, brethren, whatsoever things are true, whatsoever things are honest, whatsoever things are just, whatsoever things are pure, whatsoever things are lovely, whatsoever things are of good*

report; if there be any virtue, and if there be any praise, think on these things. (Philippians 4:8-9)

6. Watch what you eat. A low carb diet is best. Too much sugar can lead to other health problems and cause worry or even depression.

7. Stop using profanity. What comes out of your mouth will eventually program your brain. If you talk trashy, you will become trashy. It's a sliding downward fall into an unhappy place. Jesus said," *Not that which goes into the mouth defiles a man; but that which cometh out of the mouth, this defiles a man."* Matthew 15:11

"We're all capable of more than we realize. But let's face it, we're often hard on ourselves. We believe we're not good enough, or that we're failures when we have setbacks. That's the brain's way of protecting us. It's wired to take the blame for our shortcomings. But it's also the reason most people become fat, addicted or an alcoholic.

The brain is wired to be negative by default. This sets up a highly charged negative feedback loop, which can cause tremendous anxiety and depression. The solution? Change your mindset. Replace the negative things you say to yourself with more positive ones."

Here's what the Bible says about mindset. *"Therefore, if anyone is in Christ, he is a new creation; old things have passed away; behold, all things have become new.* II Corinthians 5:17 Also, *"And be not conformed to this world: but be ye transformed by the renewing of your mind, that ye may prove what is that good, and acceptable, and perfect, will of God."* Romans 12:2

This mindset shift is pictured in a poem I wrote many years ago.

The butterfly is a beautiful example of the Born-Again experience. It is a new creation that came out of a metamorphic change that took place in the life of a caterpillar.

The body of the caterpillar was changed into the body of the butterfly and it is totally different. Thus is the butterfly, never to revert back to being a caterpillar.

This is what happens to us. We are changing ever so slowly until one day when we put off mortality and soar into the realm of immortality and eternal life.

BE A BUTTERFLY

Be A Butterfly
And fly away with me.
We'll fly on the promises of God
Right into eternity

Be a butterfly
To crawl no more.
But to soar in the spirit
Above earth's mighty roar.

Be a butterfly
To fly to heights unknown.
Soaring on the wings of faith
Never more to be alone.

Be a butterfly
And fly away with me.
For God has made us knew.
At Last! At last! We are free

True change comes only after we choose to shift our mindset. If we are content to stay a caterpillar, we will never follow through with even small changes. We must decide to become a butterfly and dedicate our whole self, our entire being to the process of renewal and transformation. That may mean a complete lifestyle change.

CHAPTER NINE:
HINDRANCES TO BEING HAPPY

There are several hindrances that can defeat your quest to be happy. Here's a short list for you to consider. If the shoe fits, wear it. Better yet, toss it and get another shoe.

1. **Lifestyle Flaws**…happiness is often measured by your lifestyle. If you drink alcoholic beverages every day or stay up too late at night and get little rest, it will directly affect your mood and can even lead to depression. Running with a bad crowd, taking drugs, and dwelling on the negative things in life can also wipe away your happy attitude.

2. **Being disobedient to the known will of God** will bring a sense of guilt and, if not dealt with, will kill the joy of life in your soul.

3. **Making bad choices** will hurt you in the long run because it leads to confusion and blocks your view of a happy lifestyle.

4. **Being bored** will take the joy out of life because it turns the soul downward into the negative realm. Boredom is actually repressed anger. Face that issue and get over it.

5. **Unforgiveness** is a happiness blocker for sure because it keeps you from the blessings of God. *"For if you forgive men their trespasses, your heavenly Father will also forgive you. But if you do not forgive men their trespasses, neither will your Father forgive your trespasses."* Matthew 6:14-15.

6. **Talking negatively to yourself** is not a good idea. It will seal your fate and change your destiny because you are telling your-

self that life is bad or sad or worthless. Negative self-talk is like drinking poison.

7. **Comparing yourself to others** will surely quench the flow of happiness. You will either get a high and mighty attitude that puffs you up into pride and an egocentric behavior or you will see everyone else as better than you which will lead to a low self-esteem and/or an inferiority complex.

8. **Being pessimistic** is another hindrance to being happy because it is an outlook on life that is always negative. It causes you to seek out the sad, bad, depressed and things that are worthless in your own eyes.

9. **Fostering a critical spirit** stops the joy in your soul. If you always criticize people or events or virtually anything, you will never see life in a happy perspective. Being happy is seeing happy things. You're not God so stop judging others.

10. **Being a worry wort** is a bad thing too. It supersedes the will of God, putting you in charge of the way life should be. The problem with that is you are not God. We are to walk in faith, not worry. Faith puts God in charge and gives hope to our hearts.

11. **Low Self-esteem** says that you are not good enough; not worthy; not acceptable in society, in your family and among people in general. A good dose of scripture will fix that. There are over 3,000 promises given to God's children by God. He is a God of love, not hate. He has given us his holy Spirit to comfort us and guide us and show us the way. We are truly accepted and are joint heirs with Christ to the kingdom of God. (Romans 8:16-17)

12. **Holding on to anger** kills any hope of happiness. The Bible says that, *"Do not be eager in your heart to be angry, for* anger *resides in the* bosom *of* fools." Ecclesiastes 7:9 Don't be foolish.

13. **Mental fatigue:** the clouded, dull, sluggish state of mind that saps our concentration and ability to see others, the world, and ourselves clearly. We all "zone out" on occasion. Getting rest every night and reducing stress will do wonders in creating a positive healthy attitude and experience.

14. **Not Understanding God's Grace**...will defeat you every time. If you believe that you are saved (Accepted by God) by your obedience to the Old Testament law, you are in deep trouble. Here's why. The Bible says that *"Wherefore the law was our schoolmaster to bring us unto Christ, that we might be justified by faith." Galatians 3:24 Our justification is now by the righteousness of Jesus, not the Law.* The law was established to reveal sin. Here's another proof text. *"For by grace are ye saved through faith; and that not of yourselves: it is the gift of God: 9 Not of works, lest any man should boast"* Ephesians 2:8-9 Knowing this keeps us free from foolish religious expectations.

15. **Being unaware of evil forces**... If we are unaware of evil forces that seek our destruction, we will continually be attacked and have no defense. We are to put on the whole armor of God. (See Chapter Six)

Hear what Jesus said, *"Come to Me, all who are weary and heavy-laden, and I will give you rest"* Matthew 11:28 Jesus is the answer and his promise is to give us rest. From what? you might say. How about everything that is now keeping you from being happy?

I am sure that you can find more hindrances to being happy. There are dozens. The ones presented are the most important, in my judgment.

CONCLUSION

I have spent much time explaining the need to be saved, "Born Again". I did that because true happiness is wrapped up in salvation. Without it, there is no lasting peace or true happiness.

This book is about how to be happy. It's not rocket science. We can look into this subject and walk away with some practical knowledge and truths that are meaningful. Here's what I hope you will realize from all that has been said:

1. **True happiness starts with being a child of God**. That is where you learn about Jesus, get filled with the Holy Spirit and fellowship with your Heavenly Father. It is also a great sense of joy to be accepted. This is your eternal destiny.
2. **True happiness grows with time and circumstance.** It matures as we live life and develop a positive perspective. Small changes bring big results.
3. **Happiness is a choice**. We decide to be happy and make it happen, no matter what. Avoid the negative and reach out for the positive.
4. **Happiness is to know the Lord**. The only way to know him is to stay in the scriptures. It is there that we read about his life, miracles, power and teachings.
5. **We are most happy when we obey God's Word**. His words are calm and encouraging and he leads us to places where we can be blessed and grow in his grace.

6. **Being happy is to realize that we are a special creation of God,** created to show forth his image and likeness in the earth.
7. **We are happy when the Holy Spirit of God empowers us with his character.** It shines like the noon day sun and illuminates the darkness of our nights.

The Bible says we can be happy. Jesus says he came so we can be happy and live life to its fullest. The Holy Spirit is here with us to direct us and lead us into all truth which brings happiness. So, let's get our minds and hearts right with God and enjoy the blessings that our heavenly father wants us to have.

ABOUT THE AUTHOR:
JOHN MARINELLI

Rev. Marinelli is an ordained minister, He has formed and been pastor of one church in Wisconsin and was the pastor of another in Alabama. He has also been a youth minister and evangelism director over the years.

Rev. Marinelli has authored several other books including: "Original Story Poems", "The Art of Writing Christian Poetry," "Pulpit Poems," "Moonlight & Mistletoe," "The Mysterious Stranger," "With Eagles Wings," "Mysteries & Miracles," "It Came To Pass," Why Do The Righteous Suffer," "Believer's Handbook of battle Strategies." "Hidden In Plain Sight" "The End of The World, From The Beginning, Shadows in the Light of a Pale Moon," "Mister Tugboat" "An Elephant Named Clyde" "Morning Reign" "Times Past But Not Forgotten" and "How To Have A Victorious Christian Life."(www.marinellichristianbooks.com)

John is an accomplished Christian poet. He also dabbles in songwriting, likes to play chess, sings karaoke and goes fishing now and then. He lives in north central Florida where he enjoys a retired lifestyle with his wife and two collies.

GALLERY OF ENCOURAGING POEMS

Here are some of my Christian poetry that will bless you and encourage you to seek the Lord. I wrote them under the anointing of the Holy Spirit over the last 50-years.

AGREEING WITH GOD

We speak of things that are not,
Believing in them as though they were,
Because our Heavenly Father spoke them first,
Sending them to us in promises that never blur.

We take Him at His Word,
And listen to all He has to say.
We wrap each promise around our souls,
Until what was spoken becomes our day.

We will agree with the Lord,
Trusting that He knows best.
For only His awesome power,
Can provide our souls with rest.

"As it is written, I have made thee a father of many nations, before Him who he believed, even God who quickens the dead and calls those things that be not as though they were" Romans 4:17

Like Abraham, we also have a destiny that God has spoken into our lives. He calls it forth before it exists. Like Abraham, we are to believe, even against hope, that what God said will indeed come to be. (Romans 4:18).

ARM'S LENGTH

I hold the world at arm's length,
That its choices do not interfere.
While it does its own thing,
I watch and wait over here.

My steps must not go that way,
For it's not where I need to be.
The Lord has shown me the path,
That will lead me to my destiny.

The call of the world is strong
And pulls at me now and then.
But I know that way
Is full of sorrow and sin.

I must move on in life
Beyond their beckoning call.
It's the right thing to do,
So I do not stumble or fall.

I will not be swayed or misled
By family, friends or business deal.
Their secret thoughts are not mine,
To consider, to admire or feel.

So I keep the world at "Arm's Length"
As I journey through this life.
My faith in Jesus keeps me strong,
As I walk in His glorious light.

"Love not the world, neither the things that are in the world. If any man loves the world, the love of the Father is not in him. For all that is in the world, the lust of the flesh, the lust of the eyes and the pride of life, is not of the Father, but of the world. And the world passes away and the lust thereof: But he that doeth the will of God abides forever. I John 2:15-17

It is more important to know God and to follow after Him, than to become entangled in life's lustful traps: for if we were to gain the whole world and lose our own soul, how terrible would that be?

DON'T WORRY

Don't worry about tomorrow.
You did that yesterday.
Go on with your life
And remember always to pray.

Ask and it shall be given to you,
But this great truth you already know.
Rejoice and be happy, why? Because…
Your harvest comes from what you sow.

I will say it again and even more,
Until it becomes very very clear.
Tomorrow will take care of itself,
But worry is another word for fear.

Now here's what I want you to do.
Trust in the Lord and be of good cheer.
Drop the worry from your vocabulary
And cast out that demon of fear.

Worry is the flipside of faith. If you are walking in faith, you are free from worry. Why, because faith hopes in God and trusts that he will be there to meet your need.

TWO HOUSES

We built our homes together,
Mine upon a Rock and his in the sand.
He thought his would be all right,
But he was a foolish man.

God's wisdom showed me the way.
And what I needed to do,
But my foolish neighbor,
Never had a clue.

Then the rains came,
And the winds began to blow.
The storms beat upon our homes,
And we had nowhere to go.

We built our homes together,
My neighbor and me.
Mine is still there upon the Rock,
But his ceased to be.

Wise men and fools both suffer,
The storms that befall mankind.
But those who trust in Jesus
Will always stand the test of time.

Foundation is everything. If you build your life on the Word of God, it will last forever. That's why we strive to be obedient to the will of God. We want his destine and his blessings, no matter what the world system thinks or does.

CLUTTER

Clutter keeps the mind confused,
As images dance through the night.
Lost among those unimportant thoughts,
Are the dreams that once shined bright.

An endless parade of fear and doubt,
Crowds the mind to destroy our day.
Ever soaring on the wings of the soul,
Until it has formed an evil array.

But clutter is by one's choice,
Of those who dance to its beat.
Better to face imaginations' due
Than to fall into utter defeat.

Be Quiet!!! Is our spirit's desperate cry,
As we call upon the name of the Lord.
Silence is our heart's desired prayer,
Until our minds are again restored.

"Keep thy heart with all diligence: for out of it are the issues of life"
Proverbs 4:23

We make the final choices in life that either lead us astray or closer to the Lord. We chose what enters our hearts and fills our minds. May we always choose the path of righteousness and the way of peace.

JOHN MARINELLI

THE LORD'S LITTLE TWO BY FOUR

God has a little 2' X 4'
That rest on heaven's windowsill.
He uses it now and then,
When we stray from His will.

Sometimes we need a good "Bap";
With the Lord's little 2' X 4'
To knock out the confusion,
And help us to desire Him more.

The Lord's little 2' X 4'
Is what we sometimes need,
To get our thinking straight,
And keep our focus indeed.

The Lord's little 2' X 4'
Is fashioned from life's every trial,
So we do not stray from His will,
Or fall into an ungodly lifestyle.

"My son, despise not the chastening of the Lord; neither be weary of His correction: for whom the Lord loves, He corrects; even as a father his son, in whom he delights." Proverbs 3:11 & 12

It is a good thing to be corrected by God. We should not fear His rebuke for it is not His wrath, but rather a blessing from His love that keeps us moving on towards maturity.

I FIND MYSELF IN GOD

I find myself in God.
He is my, "Everything"
I know that He is Lord,
My Life, My Hope, My King.

I find myself in God,
Not the ways of Sin.
Nor do I look to others,
To know who I really am.

I find myself in God,
To whom I bow on bended knee.
He alone is my joy and strength
And where I want to be.

"For we are His workmanship, created in Christ Jesus unto good works, which God hath before ordained, that we should walk in them" Ephesians 2:10

Knowing that we are created in Christ Jesus gives us confidence to walk in Christ, as He walked, along a pathway of good works. It is our joy and pleasure to be like Him. In Him we move and live and have our being.

"I AM" THERE

"I AM" There,
At the end of your broken dreams,
Before the sun rises over your day,
Prior to those tear-filled streams.

"I AM" There,
Down that road of despair,
When all appears to be lost,
And no one seems to care.

"I AM" There,
Over all of life's twists and turns,
When tomorrow is all but gone,
And when you are full of concerns.

"I AM" There,
Sayeth the Lord of Host,
To bring you hope and peace,
And the power of My Holy Ghost.

"I AM" There,
To be sure you make it through,
In the midst of every trial,
To bless your life and deliver you.

"I Am" There

"All power is given unto me in heaven and earth. Go ye therefore and teach all nations, baptizing them in the name of the Father, and of the Son, and of the Holy Ghost: Teaching them to observe all things, whatsoever I have commanded you: and lo, I am with you always, even unto the end of the world." Mathew 28:18-20

The Lord is with us always. He never leaves our side, even when we leave His. In every situation, He is there. It's time to count on His presence and trust in His care.

SO LISTEN UP

I write this verse that all should know.
What I have to say is like a seed, ready to grow.
So listen up to all I have to say.
It could be the very blessing your heart needs today.

God has not given you a spirit of fear.
Instead, He has offered to dry up every tear.
He really loves you, even though you often fail.
His love and mercy follows you,
Enabling you to be the head and not the tail.

So do not worry or even fret.
That's why Jesus paid sin's awful debt.
Now go on in life to discover its victory
Knowing that Jesus has indeed set you free.

"For God hath not given us the spirit of fear: but of Power and of Love and a sound mine" II Timothy 1:7

There is nothing to fear except fear itself and that spirit has been defeated on the cross. We now have the Spirit of power and love and a sound mind. He will never leave us or forsake us. We are truly free.

JOHN MARINELLI

WINNING THE BATTLE

We must use the Word of God
To calm emotions that fray.
For the enemy never sleeps,
Until he has led us astray.

So when your emotions overflow
With feelings like depression and fear.
Know this! If you dwell in that place,
You invite the enemy to draw near.

When your emotions rage
With fiery darts aglow,
Stand in the power of the Lord,
Against its awful woe.

And if you get confused
And lost in the storm,
Put your thoughts on trial,
Rejecting all but heaven born.

You can win the battle
That rages within your soul.
By casting down imaginations,
And breaking Satan's hold.

Remember to focus on Jesus,
Holding the world at arm's length.
Lift up your head above the trial,
And the Lord will give you strength.

"For the weapons of our warfare are not carnal but mighty, through God, to the pulling down of strongholds: casting down imaginations and every high thing that exalts itself against the knowledge of God, and bringing into captivity every thought to the obedience of Christ." II Corinthians 10:3-5 The battle is in our minds and we win by putting our thoughts on trial and casting out all that oppose the knowledge of God. This is true victory.

JOHN MARINELLI

THE LIGHTHOUSE

A lighthouse is a blessing,
To the ships that toss in the sea.
For it shows them the way,
Until they can clearly see.

The rage of an angry storm,
Cannot hide its brilliant light.
Nor can its awesome furry,
Rule as an endless night.

Jesus is the lighthouse,
For those who have gone astray.
The light of His love,
Offers a new and living way.

Jesus is the lighthouse,
When fear and sickness rage.
The light of His love,
Gives hope in difficult days.

So trust in the Lord,
And look for His light.
He alone is "The Lighthouse",
That guides you through the night.

"I am the Way, the Truth, and the Life. No man cometh to the Father but by me" John 14:6

Life holds many dark nights that are full of unexpected storms. Only a deep abiding faith in Jesus Christ will get us through. He is the light of the world. His light keeps us from falling into confusion, sorrow, sickness and demonic oppression.

JOHN MARINELLI

THE WAY MAKER

Only Jesus can make a way,
Through the difficulties of life.
He alone is Lord and King,
Over life's sorrows and strife.

He is the "Way Maker,"
When there is no visible way.
He will make the way known,
As though it were the light of day.

He will make a way,
For those of humble heart.
He will clear away the rubble,
Restoring what Satan broke apart.

Jesus is the "Way Maker,"
A friend to all who are lost.
He has made the way,
Paying sin's incredible cost.

The way to the Maker,
Is through His only Son.
He alone is the "Way Maker,"
Until life's battles are won.

"Let not your heart be troubled. Ye believe in God, believe also in me. In my father's house are many mansions: If it were not so, I would have told you. I go to prepare a place for you. And if I go and prepare a place for you, I will come again, and receive you unto myself, that where I am, there ye may be also." John 14: 1-3

The Lord is prepared for any emergency. He knows the beginning from the end and has gone before us to prepare a way that we can follow until we see Him face to face.

JOHN MARINELLI

STINKING THINKING

Stinking thinking, they say,
Is bad for your health.
For it frustrates life's goals,
And denies happiness and wealth.

A right perspective is important,
As we think about everything.
It will either bring us down,
Or cause us to shout and sing.

What we think about these days,
Really does affect our life.
It can cause us to overflow with Joy,
Or fall into depression and strife.

So don't let your thinking,
Stink all the way up to heaven.
Stand in faith before God,
And get rid of that negative leaven.

"Then Jesus said unto them, take heed and beware of the leaven of the Pharisees and the Sadducees" Mathew 16:6

Someone once said, "We are what we think" The Bible says, "As a man thinks, so is he" It is important to concentrate our thinking of those things that are of good report, pure, honest and that will keep us clean of heart.

WISE MEN STILL SEEK HIM

Wise men still seek Him
Who appeared so long ago.
They come now by grace
Through faithful hearts aglow.

Wise men still seek Him
For He is their "Bread of Life."
A sustaining inner strength
Through times of sorrow or strife.

Wise men still seek Him
The Christ of Calvary.
God's only begotten Son
Crucified as Sin's penalty.

Wise men still seek Him
Jesus, God in human array.
King of kings & Lord of lords
Born to earth on Christmas Day.

"Now when Jesus was born in Bethlehem of Judea in the days of Herod the king, behold, there came wise men from the east to Jerusalem, saying, where is he that is born king of the Jews? For we have seen his star in the east and are come to worship him" Mathew 2:1-2

Seeking Jesus is the wisest thing any man, woman or child can do and when we find Him, it is our privilege to bow down and worship Him. This is our journey, our destiny and our life while on this earth.

THE ANGELS CRY HOLY

The Angels cry "Holy,"
While sorrow fills the land.
For God's Judgment Day,
Is to come upon every man.

The Angels cry "Holy,"
While mankind goes astray,
Rejecting the love of God,
To follow his own precarious way.

The Angels cry "Holy,"
Knowing the terror of the Lord,
When all who dwell in sin,
Will suddenly be destroyed.

The Angels cry "Holy,"
Waiting for all things new,
Born of the Holy Spirit,
When God's Judgment is through.

The Angels cry "Holy,"
"Holy is the Lamb,"
Waiting for the children of God,
To join "The Great I AM"

"And one cried unto another and said, "Holy, Holy, Holy, is the Lord of host: the whole earth is full of his glory" Isaiah 6:3

We serve a Holy God that deserves our reverence and homage. The angels know this and worship Him, but man, because of sin, has no real concept of his own creator.

A HIGHWAY CALLED "HOLINESS"

He places my feet on
A highway called "Holiness,"
That led my soul
To the throne of God.

Amidst the cheers of angels,
I walk, wearing His holy gown.
Onward towards heaven's throne,
While evil cast its awful frown.

My eyes were opened
That I might see.
Both the good and the evil,
That sought after me.

I walk the highway-Holiness
That crosses all of time.
Towards the throne of God,
Leaving this world behind.

"And an highway shall be there, and a way, and it shall be called, the way of holiness; the unclean shall not pass over it; but it shall be for those: the wayfaring men, though fools, shall not err therein. No lion shall be there, nor any ravenous beast shall go up thereon, it shall not be found there, but the redeemed shall walk there. And the redeemed of the Lord shall return, and come to Zion with songs and everlasting joy upon their heads: They shall obtain joy and gladness, and sorrow and sighing shall flee away. " Isaiah 35:8-10

What a privilege to walk the highway of Holiness. It is prepared especially for us, the redeemed, and it is protected from the errors of fools and the snarl of beast and especially the roar of the lion.

CALL UPON THE LORD

When your burdens overwhelm you,
Like a mighty raging sea.
Call upon the Lord, Jesus,
And He will set you free

When your heartaches are many,
And life is difficult to understand.
Call upon the Lord, Jesus.
He will come and hold your hand.

When your friends reject you,
Because you follow after Him,
Call upon the Lord, Jesus.
And keep yourself from sin.

When you fall into depression,
As though it were a giant pit.
Call upon the Lord, Jesus,
Who will restore your joyful wit.
When you're saddened by the day
Feeling lost and all alone.
Call upon the Lord, Jesus,
Who will make His way known.
When you are weary and heavy laden,
Tired from life's many tests.
Call upon the Lord, Jesus,
Who is sure to give you rest.

"Hear my cry; oh God, attend unto my prayer. From the end of the earth, I will cry unto thee, when my heart is overwhelmed: Lead me to the rock that is higher than I." Psalms 61:1-2

Calling upon the Lord in stressful times is o.k. He wants us to cry to Him and then to trust in Him to watch over His Word to perform it on our behalf.

IT CAME TO PASS

Things often come to pass,
But seldom do they ever last.
They come into our busy day,
For awhile, then pass away.

We hear their voices, loud and clear,
As they arrive and while they are here.
They speak both joy and misery,
Some to you and some to me.

We say, "It came to pass,"
Or say, "It happened so fast."
Down life's beaten path,
Comes both love and wrath.

So say goodbye to sad and blue.
To all that is now troubling you.
For things will come, only to pass,
But God's love will always last.

"And it came to pass in those days…" Luke 2:1

These are the times of our lives. We live them, some for good and some for not so good. One thing is for sure, that which comes our way, comes only to pass on by. It is not what happens that is so important, but rather what we do with what we are faced with.

Trusting in the Lord and seeking His guidance will always conquer that which comes to pass.

THE WHOSOEVER SCENARIO

The "Whosoever" is who so ever,
Not who so won't, can't or will not.
The story is as clear as a sunny day.
God offers a new and living way.

But only those who engage "free will"
To choose life, faith and obedience,
Will find salvation for their souls,
And be cleansed and made whole.

We do the choosing: to accept or deny.
That is how God set it up to be.
He made the call to life's "Whosoever",
That they could live abundantly.

"For God so loved the world, that he gave his only begotten son, that whosoever believeth in him, should not perish but have everlasting life." John 3:16

We are the "Whosoever" in John 3:16, that one day put his or her faith in Christ, believed in Him and now rest in the Lord's love and grace. We have the promise of God that He sent His Son so we could believe and have everlasting life. How great is that?

LITTLE PRISONS

Little prisons await the man with a lustful soul.
Bars of selfishness and pride create dungeons of icy cold.

Prisons of shame and jealousy fill the heart with utter despair.
Bars that separate from God and those that really care.

Stand back! While the doors are tightly closed;
Taking away your life, to wither as a dying rose.

Beware of those little prisons that trap the lustful soul.
Keep yourself free from sin through faith in the Christ of old.

Little prisons need not to be your fate.
It is your choice, Spirit or flesh to date.

"O Foolish Galatians, who hath bewitched you, that ye should not obey the truth, before whose eyes Jesus Christ hath been, evidently set forth, crucified among you? Are you so foolish? Having begun in the Spirit, are you now made perfect in the flesh?

We should always seek to dwell in the Spirit, that we would not emulate the deeds of the flesh. When we fall short, we create "little prisons" that keep us in confusion and away from the blessing of God. It's time to walk in the Spirit and break the prisons that so easily beset us.

REST MY CHILD

Rest my child, says the Lord.
Take thy peace and be restored.
I have provided, thy mouth to feed.
From the beginning, I knew your need.
Do not worry, fret or even fear,
For, my child, I am always near
To bless thy soul with love and grace,
To be with thee, face to face.
Come, my child, near to my throne.
Do not allow your faith to roam.
For those who will not believe
Can never find rest in times of need.
My Word shall see you through.
My grace I freely give to you
That you should rest, thy soul to keep,
Forever delivered from unbelief.

Resting in the Lord is the best way to stay happy. However, it requires faith and trust in God that he will be there for you when you need him. It's kind of neat to relax when fear and anxiety are knocking at your door.

A WHISPER IN THE WIND

There's a whisper in the wind
That lingers both day and night.
A champion of truth and justice,
By the power of His might.

A word in due season
That echoes from deep within.
A voice out of nowhere,
Reproving the world of sin.

Look there, in the street
And here, by the shores of the sea.
There's a whisper hidden in the wind;
A voice from eternity.

There's a calling from God.
His voice is hidden in the wind.
In a whisper, He speaks to our hearts
With the love and counsel of a friend.

Listen for the Whisper,
All who seek to know.
It is God's Holy Spirit
Telling you which way to go.

"And thine ears shall hear a word behind thee saying, This is the way, walk ye in it, when ye turn to the right hand and when ye turn to the left" Isaiah 30:21

The voice of the Lord is often a still small voice, yet always clear and it never brings confusion. His voice is like a whisper in the wind that brings a peaceful breeze to the heart. The joy of hearing His voice is to know His will and our destiny.

FRAGILE FLOWER RED

As a flower in earthen sod,
I bloom for thee, oh God.
To blossom with the turn of spring;
To be to you, a beautiful thing.

I lift my Fragile Flower Red
Upward from my earthen bed;
To draw light from God above,
Strength and peace and joy and love.

As a flower, I bloom for thee
That passersby may stop and see.
Your fragrance and beauty I am,
Flowered in grace as a man.

As a flower in earthen sod,
I bloom for thee, oh God.
Upward, I lift my head,
As a Fragile Flower Red.

"Be not conformed to this world, but be ye transformed, by the renewing of your mind, that ye may prove what is that good and acceptable and perfect will of God."

When we look to God as our source, we blossom, much like a flower that draws light from the sun. When we blossom, like a flower, we display the glory and beauty of our creator to all who care to stop and look. This is our divine destiny.

Other books by John Marinelli can be viewed and purchased at

www.marinellichristianbooks.com

www.ingramcontent.com/pod-product-compliance
Lightning Source LLC
Chambersburg PA
CBHW020425010526
44118CB00010B/428